SERGEI O. PROKOFIEFF, born in Moscow in 1954, studied fine arts and painting at the Moscow School of Art. He encountered anthroposophy in his youth, and soon made the decision to devote his life to it. He has been active as an author and lecturer since 1982, and in 1991 he co-founded the Anthroposophical Society in Russia. In Easter 2001 he became a member of the Executive Council of the General Anthroposophical Society in Dornach. He is the author of numerous books available in many languages throughout the world.

Rudolf Steiner's Sculptural Group
*A Revelation of the Spiritual Purpose
of Humanity and the Earth*

SERGEI O. PROKOFIEFF

TEMPLE LODGE

Translated from German by Simon Blaxland-de Lange

Temple Lodge Publishing
Hillside House, The Square
Forest Row, RH18 5ES

www.templelodge.com

Published by Temple Lodge 2013

Originally published in German under the title *Die Skulpturgruppe Rudolf Steiners: Eine Offenbarung des geistigen Zieles der Menschheit und der Erde* by Verlag am Goetheanum, Dornach, 2011

© Verlag am Goetheanum 2011
This translation © Temple Lodge Publishing 2013

The moral right of the author has been asserted under the Copyright, Designs and Patents Act, 1988

All rights reserved. No part of this publication may be reproduced, stored in a retrieval system, or transmitted, in any form or by any means, electronic, mechanical, photocopying or otherwise, without the prior permission of the publishers

A catalogue record for this book is available from the British Library

ISBN 978 1 906999 45 2

Cover layout by Morgan Creative featuring a photo by Michael Schnur
Typeset by DP Photosetting, Neath, West Glamorgan
Printed and bound in the UK by 4edge Ltd, Essex

In commemoration of the 150th anniversary of Rudolf Steiner's birth

Rudolf Steiner during his work on the figure of Christ (1919)

'It must be borne in mind that in the creation of this Group the whole fundamental impulse of our movement is taken into account.'[1]

Rudolf Steiner

'This sculptural Group is intended to portray what our souls should feel in the most intimate and also the deepest sense as coming from our movement.'[2]

Rudolf Steiner

'I make no claim that I shall be authoritatively believed that this is the true aspect of Christ, but this is how I see it and I have a deep inner conviction that this is the figure of Christ.'[3]

Rudolf Steiner

Contents

Introduction	1
1. The Early History of the Sculptural Group	5
2. Collaboration with Edith Maryon	11
3. The True Reality of Christ in Art	15
4. The Sculptural Group in its World-Historical Perspective. Three Aspects	21
The Group as an expression of earthly evolution	
The Group and the fourth part of the Foundation Stone Meditation	
The cosmic nature of balance	
5. The Human and Christological Mystery inherent in the Sculptural Group	27
6. The Sculptural Group and the Modern Mysteries of the Holy Grail	33
7. The Mystery of the Etherization of the Blood and the Figure of the Representative of Humanity	37
8. An Encounter with the Representative of Humanity	49
9. The Cosmic Source of the Forces of Healing	53
10. The Great Decision of Mankind	57
11. Cosmic Communion and the Essential Nature of the First Goetheanum	59
12. The Sculptural Group in the Stream of Time	65
13. The First Goetheanum and the Seventh Apocalyptic Seal	69
14. The Sculptural Group and the Legend of the New Isis	75
15. The Sculptural Group and the Being Anthroposophia	81
Three Supplements:	85
I The Sculptural Group and the Three Egos of Man	85
II The Sculptural Group and the Redemption of the Adversarial Powers	91
III The Aesthetic Germinal Foundations of the Sculptural Group	95

Appendix: From the Recollections of Heinz Müller	103
Notes	107
Bibliography	123

Introduction

There are few things in Rudolf Steiner's life with which his whole inner being was so deeply connected as was his work of creating and contemplating the wooden sculpture of the Representative of Humanity between Lucifer and Ahriman. He had initially hoped that what was perhaps the greatest work of art that he produced would take up its carefully prepared position in the eastern part of the space of the small cupola in the first Goetheanum; but through the act of arson on New Year's Eve 1922/1923 this was thwarted by the criminal hand of his opponents.

Nevertheless, the first building did not soar into the expanses of the etheric cosmos—'in which the spirit-filled wisdom of the world lives'[4]— without this central motif which, according to Rudolf Steiner, brought to expression the esoteric nature of the whole structure; for there was also the pictorial representation of this motif with its forms and colours. Nevertheless, when the building 'died into oblivion',[5] what might be called its heart was not there. Rudolf Steiner worked on it whenever he found time for this between his many journeys and the enormous quantity of his other duties. During the two years of 1923 and 1924, at the conjunction of which the greatest event of the Anthroposophical Society and movement—the Christmas Conference—took place, and also after Rudolf Steiner's decision to build the second Goetheanum, leading to the creating of a model of it, he continued to work in a focused way on carving the wooden sculpture, above all its central figure.

Two photographs that have survived from this time document in a unique way this work which Rudolf Steiner carried out for the most part alone. In them the great Christian initiate of our time can be seen carving the image of his heavenly Master. Among Rudolf Steiner's primal tasks was, without doubt, that of bringing an image of Christ to the Earth and to all human beings which was faithful to reality. And if we take seriously the fact that the true esoteric name of Christ is 'I am'[6] and bears within itself the archetype of every human ego, it can be understood that nothing should stand between a human ego and the World Ego of Christ; for in this domain alone is active the highest moral intuition of man, which becomes a spiritual communion from ego to Ego through which the human 'I' seeks and receives into itself a reflection of the 'I' of Christ.[7] What in this way can be experienced in Intuition as a direct presence of Christ in one's own ego was brought down by Rudolf Steiner through the sphere of Inspiration into that of Imagination, so as to be made manifest on the Earth itself as a visible reflection of Christ in the countenance of the Representative of Humanity. However, the original source from which *this* figure of Christ was created lay in Rudolf Steiner's ego, in his spirit. 'Rudolf Steiner saw this countenance of Christ *thus*, he said, within his spirit.'[8] It was only out of this intuitive connection of his own ego with the Christ Being that he was able to create this work of art.

However, the most difficult step on this path leading from the heights of Intuition back to the Earth, in order to make the fruits of his spiritual research accessible to all human beings, was the last one leading directly into the sense-perceptible world; for whereas the path from Intuition to Imagination lies beyond the threshold of the spiritual world, this threshold must be crossed as one takes the last, concluding step. In order that not even the slightest distortion of the fruits of spiritual research takes place at this point and creeps into the sense-perceptible world, whether in the form of words, pictures, thoughts or deeds, a quite particular spiritual power is necessary.

As no other initiate before him, Rudolf Steiner possessed not only this power but also the necessary capacity to transform what he had perceived in the spirit.[9] Thus in addition to what he researched in the spiritual world on these three levels of Intuition, Inspiration and Imagination, he was also in a position to be the bearer of initiatives in many fields of practical activity on the Earth. In this way, anthroposophical art, the two Goetheanum buildings, eurythmy, education, medicine and much else besides were inaugurated. However, the prototype for the well-nigh innumerable creative deeds that Rudolf Steiner accomplished in a short human life and made available to his fellow human beings and the world was the creation of the sculptural Group—and particularly the countenance of the Representative of Humanity.

Even though it could never be brought to completion, we stand today before this unique representation of Christ in the sculptural Group which to this day no one has managed to surpass. And although Rudolf Steiner had tried, also during his serious illness, to bring his work on the central figure of the Group—which for this reason was placed in his studio, where he also ultimately lived—to an end, he did not manage to accomplish this. Despite his growing physical frailty and the many obligations that he had—and wanted—to fulfil from his sickbed, the endeavour to finish the figure of the Representative of Humanity never forsook him. Apart from the building of the second Goetheanum as the centre of the world movement, no other task lay so close to his heart as this one. After his experience of the Christ mystery at the end of the nineteenth century and the beginning of the twentieth, which he describes in his autobiography, *The Course of My Life*, as 'having stood in spirit before the Mystery of Golgotha' (GA 28, ch. 26), the revealing of this mystery to all people of good will—not only in the form of knowledge but also through art, which makes it accessible to direct perception—was one of the most important aims of his life.

It is in this respect deeply moving to learn that, even at the very end of his earthly life, Rudolf Steiner's mind was focused on working further on the central figure of the Group whenever his physical condition permitted. No less than three days before his death, when on Friday, 27 March 1925 there was a slight improvement in his health, he immediately expressed 'the intention to get up in order to work on the Group' (GA 260a, 'Chronicle'). Marie Steiner knew this and later recalled that on this day Rudolf Steiner 'felt an improvement in his condition and wanted to get up in order to continue working on the facial expression of the sculpture' (ibid.). His concern now was not with the whole form of the Representative of Humanity (its lower part had barely been worked upon) but with the most important part—the countenance.

As already mentioned, during the whole time of Rudolf Steiner's confinement to his sickbed the sculpture of Christ stood in his studio, which also became the place of his death. This sculpture stood 'to the left at his feet'[10] in such a way that Rudolf Steiner could look at the figure of Christ day and night. The sculpture remained there also after the great initiate of the West had finally laid aside his physical sheath on 30 March 1925, in order to continue to work all the more strongly in the higher worlds for the cosmic aims of Christ.

Thus this work of art remains inseparably connected with Rudolf Steiner's destiny. In this sense Rudolf Steiner's spiritual legacy, with its urgent call to remain faithful to the fulfilling of the future tasks which the great teacher bequeathed to mankind at the behest of Christ, resides for us as his pupils in this sculptural Group, which stands today in a specially constructed space in the second Goetheanum.

1. The Early History of the Sculptural Group

Two events from the early history of the fashioning of Rudolf Steiner's great wooden sculpture, which once it was finished was to have stood in the eastern part of the small cupola of the first Goetheanum, are worthy of mention, in that they have as it were a prophetic bearing on the future arising of this unique work of art. They show at what an early stage Rudolf Steiner was living with this idea and was seeking how to make it a reality.

The first event concerns the festive opening of the first room designed in accordance with Rudolf Steiner's indications, which was that of the branch in Berlin. At that time—1909—Rudolf Steiner spoke in his dedicatory lecture of three pictures which reflect the whole evolution of mankind. First he referred to *The School of Athens* and the *Disputa* by Raphael, then he mentioned a third picture which would conclude the sequence and had still to be created.[11] In his words the first two pictures expressed 'the whole history of Greek philosophy and the whole spiritual evolution of the Middle Ages' (GA 284, 5 May 1909) in the same sense that the third picture as yet to be created out of spiritual science would have to bring to expression the spiritual nature of *our time*.[12]

It is apparent from the context of the above citation that Rudolf Steiner wanted to bring these three pictures into connection with the revelation of the Holy Trinity in the history of mankind in the sense of Lessing's *The Education of the Human Race*. In this respect *The School of Athens* corresponds to pre-Christian times,[13] which stood under the guidance of the forces of the divine Father, the *Disputa* represents the Christian epoch, which began with the Mystery of Golgotha, and the third picture which did not as yet exist at the time was to bring to expression the essential nature of the third cosmic age, that of the Holy Spirit.[14]

In the sense that it was predicted in the twelfth century by Joachim of Fiore [Flora], the third epoch actually began after the start of the Michael age in 1879 and the end of the Kali Yuga in 1899 with the founding of anthroposophy.[15] This meant that for this new epoch too a picture needed to be created which could bring its essential spiritual nature to expression. There was in this respect no contradiction in the fact that the picture, as it was uniquely exemplified, ultimately took the form of a wooden sculpture, for in the small cupola of the first Goetheanum this motif was executed in plant colours directly above the place where the wooden Group was later to stand. (See the illustration on p. 6.)

If the sculptural Group in the middle of which the form of Christ appears is brought here in connection not with the second period, that of the Son, but emphatically with that of the Spirit, this happens for a good reason; for Christ is represented in such a way that He appears here in the middle of the opposing powers, who are led through His presence, His compassion and His boundless love to take immediate flight—with the result that the eye of the observer is directed from the spiritual world towards this Christ event. Its meaning is what Christ Himself has promised in His farewell discourses in St John's Gospel, that the Spirit of Truth or Paraclete will come to human beings after the Resurrection in order to reveal the deepest secrets of the Christ mystery. Such a revelation of the Spirit is what we find in Rudolf Steiner's wooden sculpture. If, moreover, one considers the fact that the impulse of the Holy Spirit in our time is represented and mediated above all by the present Time Spirit, Michael, we can better understand in its full depth and significance why Rudolf Steiner brings this 'new Trinity' of *the Representative of Humanity between Lucifer and Ahriman* into connection with the present mission of Michael and his culture of the future.[16]

This connection with the impulse of the Spirit is further strengthened if one considers the further development of the theme of the sculptural Group in the northern rose-coloured window of the first Goetheanum. In the middle of the triptych of this window man's encounter with the etheric Christ is depicted. That this has to do with Christ's etheric appearance can be seen from the budding and sprouting plant world from which His countenance is emerging. This representation is a manifestation of His first *supersensible* revelation,[17] which can be perceived only by someone who is at this moment filled with the Holy Spirit. That this is so can be deduced from the fact that the human being in the middle part of the window is being led to this encounter with Christ by his Angel, who represents the principle of the Holy Spirit within the Third Hierarchy.[18]

On the two side windows of the triptych there is a portrayal of how Christ after the Mystery of Golgotha inclines towards Lucifer in the heights and descends into the depths of the Earth towards Ahriman, in order to redeem these two opposing powers in a Manichaean sense. This future deed no longer belongs to the epoch of the Son but to that of the Spirit. Hence Rudolf Steiner speaks for the most part about the redemption of Lucifer and only in a more cautious, though no less clear, way also about the redemption of Ahriman.[19] (See illustration on p. 9.)

The second event which prophetically relates to the arising of the sculptural Group concerns the attempt that Rudolf Steiner made several times in his lectures in 1911 to describe the countenance of Christ. One of his descriptions is reproduced here: 'If after being immersed in the spiritual-scientific conception of Christ for a long time one makes the attempt to portray Him, one arrives at a figure whose countenance expresses a quality towards which all art can endeavour to aspire and, indeed, must and will aspire; for His countenance will manifest the victory of the forces that are only in the countenance over all other forces of the human form. When people are able to fashion eyes that radiate only compassion, a mouth that is not suited for eating but only for speaking those words of truth which are the words of conscience, and when a brow can be shaped which is not fine and lofty but whose beauty lies in the clear moulding of the arch spanning the position of what we call the lotus-flower between the eyes—if all this can be achieved, it will be discovered why the prophet says: "He hath no form nor comeliness" [Isaiah 53:2]. This means that it is not beauty but a power of a different order that will have victory over decay: the figure of Christ where all is compassion, love and devotion to conscience.'[20]

In a conversation with Friedrich Rittelmeyer (1872–1938) Rudolf Steiner further clarified these observations: 'A brow unlike a modern thinker, but one upon which reverence for the deep mysteries of existence was inscribed; eyes that did not look at people as objects of observation but penetrated their very being with the ardour of devotion; a mouth: "When I saw it for the first time I had the impression that this mouth looks as though it had never taken food but has been proclaiming divine truths from all eternity."' Deeply struck by these words, Friedrich Rittelmeyer asked spontaneously—the conversation took place in the spring of 1915—whether after this description one might not also portray Christ's countenance artistically in the form of painting or sculpture. Whereupon Rudolf Steiner answered at once: 'Yes, indeed; and that is why I have given an artist in Dornach the task of making a model of Christ in accordance with my indications' (ibid.).

2. Collaboration with Edith Maryon

The artist in question was the English sculptress Edith Maryon (1872–1924).[22] As a highly gifted artist who was already well known in her native land through several exhibitions of her work, she had come to Dornach at the beginning of 1914 to collaborate in the construction of the first Goetheanum (at that time still called the 'Johannesbau' or Johannes Building). She soon, however, became an important source of help for Rudolf Steiner, above all with the preparatory work for the creation of the over nine metres high wooden Group, the carving of which was preceded by many smaller models and, finally, a large actual-size plasticine model.

Rudolf Steiner valued above all Edith Maryon's high professional ability and also her unlimited willingness to put her own artistic creativity selflessly into the background in order to serve the furtherance of his own artistic impulse. Despite her help and her active assistance, which for Rudolf Steiner were indispensable for completing the Group, there were also again and again decisive moments when he worked completely alone and dependent on his own resources. There was no one who could help him in such situations. This applied above all to the forming of the three main countenances of the wooden sculpture: those of Christ, Lucifer and Ahriman. Assya Turgeniev (1890–1966) reported: 'Here [in the neighbouring studio[23]], he worked in greater seclusion on the central figure.' And she adds: 'Our preliminary work gained significantly in its character and expressive power through the inner experience which guided his hands.'[24] The reason for this becomes clear at once if one bears in mind that here for the first time in world history actual portraits of these three beings could be made out of a purely spiritual perception, which could be achieved only be someone who, as a modern Christian initiate of the first rank, himself beheld them in the higher worlds.

The following little episode indicates how difficult it was at times for Edith Maryon to become accustomed to direct spiritual realism of this kind and its spiritual immediacy, which was without precedent in the whole history of art. When Edith Maryon in Rudolf Steiner's absence once herself carved a Christ figure, he was—on returning from a lengthy lecture tour—visibly alarmed by this but said with a friendly humour which bridged the painfulness of the whole situation: 'This English lord is not my Christ, however' (ibid.). Whereupon he altered the whole form, but especially the countenance, and then finally finished it in his own way. The manner in which Edith Maryon took Rudolf Steiner's friendly but nonetheless clear criticism says much for her greatness. Assya Turgeniev says in her reminiscences: 'For all her artistic gifts, it came as a matter of course to her to be merely a pupil, the hand which was there to serve Rudolf Steiner' (ibid.).

A similar problem also becomes apparent in the sculptural eurythmy figures which Edith Maryon made independently from plaster, if one compares them with the wooden figures that she carved in accordance with Rudolf Steiner's sketches and indications. The latter are even today, after a hundred years, timeless and wholly modern works of art. The former are—for all their artistic skill and beauty—quite obviously characteristic of their time, so that any art connoisseur will immediately identify them as beautiful examples of art nouveau from the early twentieth century.

As for how they came to be made, the eurythmy figures came into being in 1919 at the suggestion of Edith Maryon. Rudolf Steiner warmly welcomed this idea. However, her first attempts to draw the figures and then also to fashion them sculpturally went in a totally different direction from how Rudolf Steiner had imagined. Thus he had to intervene quite decisively here as well. 'The idea of the figures came, in the first place, from Miss Maryon, but the way they have been made is wholly in accordance with what I consider to be right for the laws of eurythmy' (GA 307, 17 August 1923). And during his memorial address in Dornach he expressed it still more clearly: 'The idea [from Edith Maryon] was an extraordinarily fruitful one. The form of the actual figures had to be completely changed' (GA 261, 3 May 1924). See the illustrations on p. 13.

And so on the many occasions when Rudolf Steiner received guests or his pupils in the studio where he worked on the central figure of the sculptural Group, the Representative of Humanity, he would say to them as he pointed to the countenance of Christ (whether to the actual-size bust of 1915 or to the gradually arising wooden figure): 'This is how I see Him in the spiritual world.'[25] And in the lecture of 29 June 1921 about the figure of the Representative of Humanity he added: 'One can imagine it as the Christ. I have fashioned it as a Christ figure wholly out of my intuitive perception.'[26]

The Appearance of Christ in the Etheric and the Being Anthroposophia

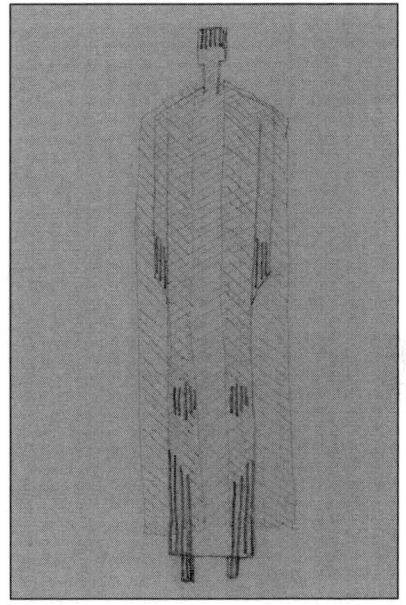

3. The True Reality of Christ in Art

At this point one needs to stop and think about what it really means that the only *authentic image of Christ* that has existed hitherto was fashioned at the beginning of the twentieth century, after the first quarter of the consciousness-soul age had run its course and out of the forces of this soul faculty. If in our time we study this unique countenance more closely, especially as it was manifested in the bust that Rudolf Steiner sculpted with his own hands at Easter 1915 (see illustration on p. 14), we can also sense what Friedrich Rittelmeyer expressed in the following words: 'But then one began to realize more and more clearly that it was simply impossible to have any different conception of Christ. In its sublime purity this figure of Christ was far and away superior to all others ... Was there not here an element of the promise: I will come again and abide with you?'[27] Over 95 years after this image was sculpted and especially against the background of the tragic events of the twentieth century and in the light of the appearance of the etheric Christ, its power has distinctively increased.

Every person who in our time and in the future—according to Rudolf Steiner, for at least three thousand years—has had or will have the good fortune to encounter the etheric Christ can recognize the full significance of this work of art, because this countenance is a familiar part of his own spiritual experience. From what has been said, however, the opposite is also true—that a meditative contemplation of the countenance of the Representative of Humanity, above all of the sculptural bust referred to, is eminently suited to prepare people today for an encounter with the etheric Christ and can even lead them to such a meeting.

The explanation that Rudolf Steiner gives for a certain asymmetry in the countenance of the Representative of Humanity, especially in the region of the brow, relates this to the etheric domain; for immediately after one has risen from the physical world of the senses to the etheric aspect of the spiritual world, everything becomes livingly asymmetrical. In this connection Rudolf Steiner says initially about the spirit being at the top left and then about the countenance of the Representative of Humanity: 'There is one thing that you will notice about this being, even though it comes to expression only through certain hints: you will see that whenever spiritual forms are the object of our consideration an asymmetrical element must make its influence felt ... As soon as one ... enters the spiritual domain, the etheric body works in a distinctly asymmetrical way' (GA 181, 3 July 1918). And then he continues: 'In this case [the central figure] the head also had to be made somewhat asymmetrical ... You will only see from the completed head of the central figure how to conceive of this artistically [he is referring here mainly to the formation of the brow]' (ibid.). And in another lecture, where he was similarly speaking about the asymmetry of the countenance of the central figure, Rudolf Steiner indicates that this is a particular expression of the inner mobility of this face, which manifests in a certain sense more of an etheric than a physical law: 'And this comes to expression in that a greater inner mobility had to be introduced into the main figure than would [otherwise] be appropriate for a human being' (GA 157, 10 June 1915).

How this way of portraying Christ and the two adversaries arose was explained by Rudolf Steiner in answer to the question of the young Waldorf teacher Heinz Müller (1899–1968). First he spoke about how the figures of the adversaries came into being: 'Present-day humanity would need to try to develop clear conceptions of the adversarial forces and in this way wrest their power from them. For this reason he had also endeavoured—so he said—to make his portrayal of them as exact as possible in all its details. In this way he ensured that his figures were as much of a likeness as possible. As his guest [Heinz Müller] was evidently highly surprised at these words, he followed them up with the further startling remark that he had compelled both Ahriman and Lucifer to sit for him as models.[28] With Ahriman he succeeded only after applying a considerable degree of force, whereas Lucifer adapted himself relatively easily to this situation ... While these words were being spoken I was filled with marvelling and reverential thoughts about the greatness of the spirit who was able to say such things as though as a matter of course.'[29] Especially what Müller goes on to report about this conversation clearly shows the high level of Rudolf Steiner's initiation; for he adds that 'he [Rudolf Steiner] had kept Ahriman confined to this chair until he had finished his study. Then *he*—Rudolf Steiner—ended the session, but Ahriman sought revenge by destroying the great crimson window on the western façade of the Goetheanum. At that time this window developed a crack from top to bottom.'[30] Rudolf Steiner also mentioned this fact in a lecture for members, though without entering into such startling details: 'I made the attempt to fashion *these three figures*—we may say something of this sort in such an intimate circle as this—to the best of my ability as true likenesses' (GA 159, 15 May 1915).[31] From this one can be quite certain that no other person—not even Edith Maryon—could have helped Rudolf Steiner in this; for these sculptural portraits could only be fashioned out of a direct spiritual perception, which is why the spiritual power of an initiate of the first rank was necessary in order to exert a commanding authority over the adversaries.[32]

This applies to an even greater degree to the countenance of Christ Himself, the painting (in the cupola of the first Goetheanum) and sculpting of which presented Rudolf Steiner initially with almost insuperable difficulties, not only as the artist executing these works of art but above all as the initiate who was beholding them. These difficulties which the initiate encountered as he sought to record the countenance of the living Christ in the spiritual world for a work of art, to condense it into an imagination and then engrave it into the material substance of the physical world (wood, plaster or plasticine),[33] were also described by him in the conversation with Heinz Müller: 'Then Rudolf Steiner also spoke about the similarity between his study and the countenance of Christ. If one were to encounter Him in the spiritual world, one's first impression would be that His countenance would change to a surprisingly strong degree with every thought, feeling and will impulse ... Now that His Being has been living freely in the etheric heights independent of the body of Jesus of Nazareth, this constant changing of His countenance and, indeed, of His whole form has further intensified.' And then Rudolf Steiner adds these decisive words: 'Nevertheless ... both the sculpture and the coloured portrayals of the Representative of Humanity [the reference is to the fresco in the small cupola above the intended position of the sculptural Group] have been wrought in such a way that one would immediately recognize Him if one were to meet Him. Thus here too one may speak absolutely of a kind of true likeness.'[34]

Herein lies the key to why, in the various descriptions that he gave of it in lectures over the years, Rudolf Steiner constantly interpreted the wooden sculpture in different ways. Some particularly characteristic examples among many will be given here. Thus he says in 1923 in connection with the description of the Easter imagination that the initiate would be able directly to behold the figure of the Representative of Humanity, establishing the balance between the adversarial forces, in the spiritual world both now and in the future. He added in more precise terms, clarifying his description with a big coloured picture on the blackboard, that what he was presenting was 'the figure of Christ freeing Himself from the weight of matter ... as we have shown here [in the Goetheanum] in painting and sculpture ... So there appears before our eyes, between the ahrimanic and the luciferic forms, Christ in His Resurrection form as the Easter picture' (GA 229, 7 October 1923)—not only as He will have appeared to the disciples on Easter morning at the Turning Point of Time but at the same time as an image of Christ that is 'born out of cosmic events in the course of the year' (ibid.). This is the *Risen* Christ who since the Mystery of Golgotha can be found in the spiritual aura of the Earth at any time—or, as one could also say, in His *eternal present*.

Rudolf Steiner did, however, also speak in quite different ways about the countenance of the Representative of Humanity. Thus, for example, he says in a lecture that in the sculptural Group Christ was actually portrayed as He appeared in Palestine at the Turning Point of Time. This contrasts with most canonical representations where Christ is depicted with a beard.[35] In a slide lecture given in Bern Rudolf Steiner refers to this as follows: 'The painted head of Christ between Ahriman and Lucifer [this also applies to the central figure of the sculptural Group] . . . You see that the attempt has been made to portray Christ without a beard; images of Christ have actually only had beards since the end of the fifth or sixth centuries. Of course no one needs to believe me, but *this is the Christ as He appeared to me in spiritual vision*, and He must here be portrayed without a beard.'[36]

There also exist indications by Rudolf Steiner that the sculptural Group reflects a specific scene from the earthly life of Christ Jesus, which is known as the temptation in the wilderness (although in this case in accordance with the Fifth Gospel). Thus according to the images of the Akashic Record the three temptations took place in such a way that it was only Lucifer who approached Christ Jesus during the temptation on the mountain; on the pinnacle of the temple Lucifer and Ahriman acted together; and lastly, in the case of the temptation to turn stones into bread, Ahriman acted alone. Accordingly the opposing powers are likewise divided in a compositional sense in the wooden sculpture: at the top Lucifer alone plunges into the abyss; Lucifer and Ahriman work together to the left of the central figure; and Ahriman alone is at the bottom in his kingdom beneath the Earth after the third unsuccessful assault.[37] Rudolf Steiner refers as follows to the relationship of the sculptural Group to Christ's temptations in the wilderness: 'A nine-metre-high sculptural Group made of wood, where the Representative of Humanity was portrayed *being tempted* by Lucifer and Ahriman, may serve as something where everything that has lived in forms and could be said or artistically depicted in the Goetheanum has been brought together' (GA 84, 9 April 1923).[38]

As a third, and final, example, the words where Rudolf Steiner relates his artistic creation to the Baptism in the Jordan, or to be precise the moment immediately after it, may be cited: 'At the centre of this Group a figure will stand as, I should say, the representative of the highest aspect of humanity that could develop on the Earth. Hence one will be able to experience this figure representing the culmination of human evolution on Earth as the Christ who dwelt for three years of earthly evolution in the body of Jesus of Nazareth' (GA 159, 18 May 1915). And then he says more precisely: 'The particular task will be to fashion this figure of Christ in such a way that on the one side one will be able to see how the Being concerned lives in a human earthly body but nevertheless how in every expression, in everything belonging to its nature, this earthly body is spiritualized by what *in the thirtieth year* of life entered into this earthly body from spiritual heights as the Christ' (ibid.).

This moment, of which John the Baptist was able to give his unique testimony, must be imagined quite concretely as a fact of world history. A human being—Jesus of Nazareth—whom John had known well for years if not decades through their shared experience of early childhood,[39] and then through their later meetings and conversations in the Essene community,[40] steps into the water of the River Jordan. And after the Baptism the one who steps out of the water is still a human being, but now bearing in himself the highest, most all-encompassing and, indeed, the central Being of the spiritual world; for from this moment onwards the Son of God begins to shine through the Son of Man. This came to expression above all in that thenceforth the countenance of this earthly being was the purest expression of wonder, love and conscience and, hence, surpassed everything that one can imagine in connection with a human countenance and its means of expression.[41] Portraying this transformation artistically was also a task associated with the central figure of the sculptural Group. For the first time in the history of mankind the reality of Christ—which lies beyond time—from the spiritual world was brought into the earthly world through a work of art and, hence, became visible to all people in the form of the Representative of Humanity.

4. The Sculptural Group in its World-Historical Perspective: Three Aspects

Every true work of art is multi-dimensional. Thus the following aspects are neither complete nor do they claim to do justice to the sculptural Group in every respect.

The Group as an expression of earthly evolution

From the standpoint of spiritual history, the meaning of the sculptural Group encompasses the whole of earthly evolution, of which Rudolf Steiner says that its first part bore luciferic characteristics while the second has a more ahrimanic character. The incarnation of Lucifer in the third millennium before Christ in China and the imminent incarnation of Ahriman in North America at the beginning of the third millennium form the centres of gravity of this evolution. (See GA 191, 4 November 1919.)

Because of their intense efforts to oppose Christ, the two adversaries also frequently work together. Thus they unite their forces at the turn of every millennium in order to manifest their opposition to the Christ impulse. (See GA 286, 7 March 1914.) This is happening in our present time, because we are still living in the transitional phase of the third millennium.[42] All this has a direct connection with the essential nature of the wooden sculptural Group and above all with that aspect that links it with the Turning Point of Time. For at that time—because this was no mere transition between two millennia but between the two halves of earthly evolution—the combined influence of the opposing forces was considerably stronger. In the three motifs of the sculptural Group that surround the central figure, Lucifer above, Ahriman below and Lucifer and Ahriman working together on the left side, we find all three lines of attack of the adversaries, as they were active before the Mystery of Golgotha, at the Turning Point of Time and in the time after it and as they continue to work today. The central part of the sculptural Group portrays their vanquishing by the Representative of Humanity, which opens up the way of fulfilling the purpose of earthly evolution as a whole.

The Group and the fourth part of the Foundation Stone Meditation

With respect to the mystery history of humanity the wooden sculpture also has a close connection with the fourth part of the Foundation Stone Meditation. This has to do with the shepherds and the kings, who at the Turning Point of Time had the task of preparing the incarnation of Christ on the Earth. The shepherds represented more the southern mysteries, in which the pupil sought access to the spiritual world by immersing himself in his own inner being; whereas the kings bore within themselves the secrets of the northern mysteries, in which the pupil aimed to attain a relationship to the higher worlds behind the veil of sense perceptions. Rudolf Steiner referred to Gautama Buddha as the highest and representative initiate for the stream of the shepherds, and to Zarathustra as having a comparable relationship to that of the kings. He also said of them that the former had to overcome the seductions of Lucifer on the path to his enlightenment (the demon Mara in the Buddhist tradition), whereas Zarathustra had to wage a long battle against Angra Mainyu (Ahriman). What happened by way of an example with these two great initiates was also enacted in the case of every pupil of the respective mysteries. For in order to approach the spiritual world through immersing oneself in one's own soul, one has at least to a certain extent to overcome Lucifer within one's own being; and in order to be able to behold the spirit of the cosmos behind the tapestry of sense perceptions there is a corresponding need to overcome Ahriman.

The union of the two streams, which at the Turning Point of Time were still separated, became possible through Christ's appearance on the Earth. Rudolf Steiner speaks of this in the following words: 'In Christ one has a God who can be found both in the outer world *and* in the inner world' (GA 113, 28 August 1909; italics Rudolf Steiner). Thus Christ stood spiritually at the end of every path of the mysteries. However, only through His appearance on the Earth was He able to bring the two paths into a higher unity.[43]

At this point one needs to recall that Rudolf Steiner connects the meeting with the lesser and the Greater Guardian with initiation into these two kinds of mysteries, which in themselves represent the two great post-Atlantean migration streams of mankind (the southern and the northern). One encounters the lesser Guardian when immersing oneself in one's own soul, and as one reaches lovingly into the outer world one meets with the Greater Guardian. From this it becomes possible to understand the basis on which the connection with *both* Guardians is forged on the modern path of schooling.[44] For the way that Rudolf Steiner describes the encounter with them in the last two chapters of his book *Knowledge of the Higher Worlds: How is it Achieved?* (GA 10) is that it only became possible as a consequence of the Mystery of Golgotha; and this has a direct connection with the content of the sculptural Group.

The cosmic nature of balance

The enigmatic figure of the being in the upper left corner of the Group also has a particular significance in this respect. It appears on the Earth as an emissary of cosmic expanses, manifesting itself out of a rocky background. Here, too, there is a reference to something of a future orientation. Thus Rudolf Steiner speaks of how from our time onwards spiritual beings (the 'good spirits') from other planets and even from a more distant cosmos will with increasing frequency come to the Earth. But in order that their arrival on the Earth can be of help to human evolution, they must be received by human beings in a way that is possible only upon the foundation of a preparation through spiritual science. (See GA 204, 13 May 1921.) Rudolf Steiner once spoke along these lines about this enigmatic figure. Assya Turgeniev, who was present at the time, recalls: 'A being "which has nothing to do with the Earth" appeared as an "observer" at the top on the left of the rocky mountain mass; "this being comes from the cosmos and observes earthly happenings".'[45]

This enigmatic spirit-figure also, therefore, has a connection with what Rudolf Steiner says regarding the possibility of informing oneself about the meaning of earthly evolution from human works of art. He describes in a lecture how an extraterrestrial being, for example 'a spirit from Mars', might come down to the Earth and would quite naturally find much there that was incomprehensible. But if this being were taken to see *The Last Supper* by Leonardo da Vinci, it would immediately be able to discern from it the entire meaning of the Earth. (See GA 132, 7 November 1911.) The encounter of such an extraterrestrial being with the sculptural Group would be of no less significance, in that this work of art would make manifest to it the most important mysteries of man's being not only from the epoch of the Son but above all from that of the Holy Spirit.

This does not, however, in any way exclude another interpretation of this cosmic being, that its task is to call forth in people the quality of true humour, which according to Rudolf Steiner can have a thoroughly serious character; for this quality is needed not only inwardly to free oneself from the effects of an encounter with the adversarial forces but also to avoid a tendency to wallow in feelings or sentimentality when contemplating what is highest (the central figure).

In the process of the Group's creation the adding of this being should be viewed in connection with the observation of Mieta Waller (1883–1954) that the sculpture was not as yet properly balanced but apparently inclined to one side. ' "Herr Doctor," she called out spontaneously, "the Group statue is leaning too much to the right, it is not in proper balance."—"You are right," he answered after a brief reflection." '[46] And the following morning Rudolf Steiner added to the model the enigmatic figure, which through the asymmetry of its face manifests a strong relationship to the etheric cosmos.

A further effect of this being is revealed from this history: it is like the secret guardian of the principle that brings to manifestation the main idea of the entire sculpture—balance. Because of this it has a quite particular relationship to the Christ Being, who represents precisely this quality in the cosmos and in man. Hence this cosmic being is at the same time the witness of the unbroken presence and influence of Christ in the spiritual sphere of the Earth in the sense of His words: 'And lo, I am with you always, to the close of the age' (Matthew 28:20).

★

The power of balance—in its cosmic and earthly aspects—that is concentrated in the sculptural Group was to permeate the totality of the first Goetheanum as the architectural principle that formed and radiated from it. Rudolf Steiner explains the nature of this formative power above all in a lecture where he enters at some length into the various aspects of the influence of Lucifer and Ahriman in man and in the cosmos. Thus among the manifold influences of the adversarial forces he also emphasizes that wherever there is a straight line the ahrimanic forces are active, and wherever a curved line appears it is more a sign of the involvement of the luciferic powers.

If one considers the architectural concept of the first Goetheanum from this standpoint, one recognizes a form that is the result of a perfect balance between a cross, which arises from two straight lines at right angles to one another, and two intersecting and overlapping circles.[47]

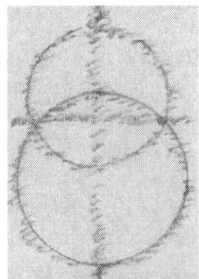

Rudolf Steiner then transfers this principle of balance that arises between curved and straight lines to the building as a whole and describes it from this perspective in the following words: 'Look at the forms of our building: everywhere the straight line is translated into the curve, balance is sought, everywhere the attempt is made to dissolve rigid into flowing forms and to achieve peace in movement, but a peace that is once more set in motion. That is why our building has such a spiritual quality ... Thus our building has become a means of creating balance in the universe which has managed to raise itself out of the kingdom of Ahriman and the kingdom of Lucifer. Everything culminates in the central figure of our Group, in this Representative of Humanity where everything of a luciferic and ahrimanic nature is obliterated' (GA 184, 21 September 1918).

On looking more closely one indeed finds this formative principle everywhere in the first Goetheanum: in the upright power of the bearing columns on which the two huge cupolas rest; or in the diversely finished forms of the architraves which, however, also manifest a lineal direction in the dynamic thrust of their movement. Moreover, the aforesaid principle of balance between the ahrimanic and the luciferic can be discerned in many of the smaller details of the inner form of the building.

Thus one gradually lives into the unique form-language of this building and comes thereby to an experience of the purely Christian element active within it, which is revealed ever more clearly to the attentive observer both from the building as a whole and from all its details. It is solely because of this that the nature of the first Goetheanum's construction is archetypally Christian. The first Goetheanum was wholly imbued with the Christ impulse; and the figure of the Representative of Humanity in the sculptural Group bears a unique witness to its presence in the building.

5. The Human and Christological Mystery inherent in the Sculptural Group

Because the sculptural Group is concerned with the Representative of Humanity, an aspect of it which has a particular importance is the insight that it affords into human nature, which is also associated with the deepest mysteries of anthroposophical Christology. One can experience the manifold elements of the Group as an expression of the threefold being of man and also as a revelation of the two paths between which mankind must freely decide in our time and, hence, determine the further course of earthly evolution. In order that such a decision may be understood more clearly, the following should be taken into account. One of the greatest spiritual-scientific discoveries made by Rudolf Steiner is without doubt the threefold nature of the human body, which he published for the first time in 1917 in the appendices to the book *Von Seelenrätseln* ('The Riddles of the Soul', GA 21). This has to do with the three bodily systems that are diffused throughout the human body as a whole but nevertheless have their respective centres in the systems of the head, the heart and the limbs.

In the lecture of 28 November (GA 194) Rudolf Steiner describes how in people today the luciferic spirits work above all in the region of the head, whereas the ahrimanic spirits are active in the region of the limbs and metabolism: 'Man is placed in the world at present in such a way that his head is supported by Lucifer and his metabolic wisdom—that of his limbs—by Ahriman.' That this is so is due in both cases to the activity of Michael in the spiritual world. For it was he who, at the beginning of human evolution (on Lemuria), cast the luciferic spirits down from the higher regions to the realm of human beings, with the result that they could be tempted. 'Thus it is Michael who sent his opponents to human beings in order that, by receiving this adversarial luciferic element, man might be gifted with his reason' (GA 194, 22 November 1919).

In the second half of the nineteenth century Michael brought about something similar with a certain body of ahrimanic spirits (even with Ahriman himself[48]), whom Rudolf Steiner refers to as the spirits of darkness. They too were cast down by Michael from the spiritual world of human beings, where they ultimately became entrenched in man's limb and metabolic system.[49] By virtue of their earthly organism human beings were subjected from both these directions to a constant, twofold temptation: by Lucifer from above, from the region of the head, and by Ahriman from below, from the depths of the limbs and metabolic system—for in the human organism the subterranean forces are associated first and foremost with the metabolic system.

In the sculptural Group the activity of Lucifer in the upper region and of Ahriman in the sub-earthly domain is indicative of this state of affairs. The efforts of the adversarial powers to join forces in our time are portrayed in the motif on the left side of the sculptural Group, which reflects their union in the middle region of man's being where the rhythmical activity of the heart and the lungs belong. Thus Lucifer and Ahriman, each in his own way, want to conquer the domain of the human heart, in order there to 'reach out their hands' to one another, as comes to expression in the motif on the left side of the Group. But as man's ego is centred in this region of his being,[50] it is for this reason—to the extent that the adversaries succeed in this—taken hold of by the forces of opposition and drawn into the 'eighth sphere' or the sphere of evil.

What is this sphere of evil? It consists of the imaginative substance of Old Moon, which was illegitimately preserved by the luciferic spirits and then imbued with earthly substantiality by the ahrimanic powers. As a result, this sphere arose as 'a bogus element in the universe' (GA 254, 18 October 1915), as something that belongs neither to the Old Moon nor to the present Earth but consists of 'condensed imaginations' (ibid.) which function like 'spectres', that is, a situation is created where spiritual substance ('imaginations') appears in a physical, sense-perceptible form ('condensed'). In this way it becomes a place where everything can be found which is useless for the present Earth evolution.[51] It becomes the gathering place for all residues which will subsequently be separated by the higher powers from the Earth at its transition to Jupiter.[52]

Before it comes to this point, however, the luciferic and ahrimanic powers are trying through their *combined* efforts to bring the whole of earthly evolution under the control of this sphere: 'No less a prospect looms as a consequence of this intention of Lucifer *and* Ahriman than that the whole evolution of humanity may be allowed to disappear into the eighth sphere, so that this evolution would take a different course' (GA 254, 18 October 1915).

So this *eighth* sphere created by Lucifer and Ahriman specifically in opposition to the Spirits of Form (Elohim) as the rightful leaders of the Earth establishes itself alongside the rightly advancing *seven* stages of evolution stretching from Old Saturn to the future Vulcan.

However, this is not the full extent of the dark mystery of this sphere. For Rudolf Steiner indicates that it can become a gateway for assaults of the Asuras upon mankind, which make themselves perceptible whenever Lucifer and Ahriman join forces and thereby prepare the ground for man to come under the sway of this third power of evil.[53] And what has fallen prey to the asuric powers will be conclusively lost to subsequent earthly evolution: 'What has succumbed to the Asuras will be irredeemably lost' (GA 107, 22 March 1909). This applies above all to man's ego, which the Asuras seek to destroy.[54]

In contrast to this there is the possibility that is available to every human being since the Mystery of Golgotha: of receiving Christ freely and consciously into one's own heart, so that the power of Christ that accordingly becomes present there as the fount of love and balance within man can drive away the adversarial forces.[55] This is precisely what is portrayed in the central motif of the wooden sculpture: Christ actively present in the human heart, causing Lucifer to leave the head and Ahriman the limbs. This is why Lucifer plunges down with broken wings into the cosmic abyss and Ahriman is bound by veins of gold in the depths of the Earth.[56]

Rudolf Steiner describes Christ's connection with man's middle system in the following words: 'By what means has inner logic, inner wisdom and a capacity of inner orientation entered into this middle part of our human nature? Through the Christ impulse, through what has pervaded earthly culture as a result of the Mystery of Golgotha. There is a spiritual-scientific anatomy which shows us what a culture of the head is [where Lucifer is active], which shows us what a culture of the metabolism is [where Ahriman is active] and which also shows the nature and needs of that sphere of our organism which lies between the two. *Being imbued with the Christ impulse is an intrinsic part of human nature*' (GA 194, 28 November 1919).

From this emerges the decisive question of modern times: will human beings consciously and freely open their hearts to the Christ impulse in order gradually also to overcome the adversaries in their heads and limbs—or will they reject the Christ impulse? Were the latter to occur, the whole of earthly evolution would be guided in the direction portrayed in the motif on the left, where Lucifer and Ahriman join forces in the heart region, thus opening up the gateway to the eighth sphere; for it always opens up when the adversaries are working together.

Man would in such a case be in danger of his soul likewise disappearing into the eighth sphere. 'It would be the richest prize for Lucifer *and* Ahriman if they could succeed in capturing an entire soul; for such a soul would thereby disappear into the eighth sphere for the duration of Earth evolution' (GA 254, 18 October 1915). And because the ego dwells in the soul during the Earth incarnation, it would also disappear into the eighth sphere.

It is particularly suggestive in this sense that Rudolf Steiner speaks often and at some length about freedom, which is directly associated on Earth with the ego and its further development: 'The endeavour of Lucifer *and* Ahriman is to drag man's free will into their eighth sphere' (ibid.). Whereas the Representative of Humanity, from whom the adversaries flee, is opposed to this destruction of the ego brought about by the collaboration of Lucifer and Ahriman (depicted in the left-hand motif). Because of this He is able to defend the human ego from being assailed by the Asuras. Christ Himself is then present within man as is expressed by the words of St Paul, 'Not I, but Christ in me',[57] words which Rudolf Steiner related initially to the entire building and somewhat later to the sculptural Group.

Thus he spoke in Dornach on 20 September 1914 in recollection of the laying of the building's foundation stone a year before: 'May it be to our lasting benefit that in these forms [of the Goetheanum] one sees how the Spirit which brought its tidings to the Earth through the Mystery of Golgotha streams through our forms, takes hold of the forms and imbues them with the Christ impulse, so that the soul may be filled with the consciousness that is expressed in the words: Not I, but Christ in me! Even if it represents only imperfectly what is wanted, may this building achieve at least in a small way what is its intention: to make an impression on those who enter it such that it is not I, not my own being that makes an impression on the eye through the outer forms but the Christ would speak ... And this building shall be "the mouth"!'[58]

What was said here with respect to the Goetheanum as a whole was related half a year later—after Rudolf Steiner had himself fashioned the first model of the Group out of plasticine—to the future sculptural Group, in which 'everything that lived [in the building] by way of its forms was brought together' (GA, 9 April 1923). Rudolf Steiner expressed this in the following words: 'Man must on the one hand reject the luciferic principle and, on the other, the ahrimanic principle, but he must stand firm through the cultivation of what Paul referred to in the words: "Not I, but Christ in me"' (GA 159, 18 May 1915). Here the words 'not I' or 'not my own being' can be related to the motif on the left side of the Group or to what must be overcome in man if he wants to ascend to higher regions, and 'in me' to the adversarial forces fleeing in both an upwards and a downwards direction, thus freeing the place in the middle—in the realm of the ego—for the constant presence of Christ within man.

The Human and Christological Mystery inherent in the Sculptural Group   31

Rudolf Steiner's observation about the inner relationship of the sculptural Group to the words of St Paul reveals to us what is perhaps the most profound mystery of this highly important work of art. For if we bear in mind that in the first Goetheanum it was as though an overall summary of the whole of anthroposophy had become visible and that the sculptural Group was, moreover, to form the building's spiritual centre, enabling people today to gain a new, spiritual understanding of Christianity, we may with justice also directly connect the following words of Rudolf Steiner with the esoteric essence of the Group: 'It forms part of the inner mission of the spiritual [anthroposophical] world-stream to prepare human beings to become so mature in soul that an ever-increasing number of people will be able to take into themselves a copy of the Ego Being of Christ Jesus ... Anyone who acquires a spiritual understanding of Christianity and experiences it inwardly will be taking steps towards enabling a copy of the Ego of the Christ Jesus individuality to be woven into his ego either in the present or in a later incarnation' (GA 109, 7 March 1909).

These words were spoken in 1909, four years before the laying of the foundation stone of the first Goetheanum in Dornach, when they were also given an artistic form. For their first part can be directly related to the building as an anthroposophical *Gesamtkunstwerk* (unified work of art), and the second directly to the sculptural Group, which presents the essential nature of the new, spiritual Christianity to people today and at the same time enables them to understand it.

Some of the qualities of the sculptural Group referred to in this book also point in this direction. Thus Rudolf Steiner speaks further about the mystery of the copies of Christ's Ego: 'But when people will [through anthroposophy] be increasingly well prepared to receive Christ's Ego, it will imbue their souls to an ever-increasing degree. They will then evolve to the level where their great model, Christ Jesus, used to be. Only in this way will human beings learn to understand the extent to which Christ Jesus is the great model for humanity' (GA 109, 11 April 1909).

In other words: through receiving Christ man will fully experience what is said in the book *An Outline of Occult Science* of Christ as the 'sublime earthly ideal of earthly humanity' (GA 13). And this is what Rudolf Steiner says of the Representative of Humanity: 'In the middle of this Group a figure will stand who could be described as the representative of the highest human qualities that could develop on the Earth' (GA 159, 18 May 1915).

Thus the central figure of the Group was perceived by Rudolf Steiner himself through the Ego of Christ which he received as a copy into his own ego⁵⁹ and then transformed into a work of art, so that this mystery can now become visible to all people. Since then this figure can also become for others a path on which they can inwardly unite themselves—even 'identify'—with it,⁶⁰ in order to prepare themselves for the receiving of a copy of Christ's Ego. For the central figure of the sculptural Group is the Christ as He can be seen by a human being with the spiritual eye of Christ Himself, that is, out of the copy of His Ego. Hence in the same lecture Rudolf Steiner goes on to say that those who are inspired by and imbued with Christ's Ego and whom he calls 'the Christians of the future' will see something additional in Christ, namely His whole cosmic power and glory: 'They will understand not only the Christ who has passed through death but also the triumphant Christ of the Apocalypse who soared aloft into the spiritual fire,⁶¹ whose coming has already been proclaimed' (GA 109, 11 April 1909). In the sculptural Group Rudolf Steiner indeed portrayed such a Christ triumphing over the adversaries, that is, 'in the spiritualized fire in which Christ appeared to Paul' (ibid.).⁶² Hence Rudolf Steiner indicates in this context that those individuals who receive a copy of Christ's Ego 'will increasingly change from being people of Saul to being people of Paul and will behold a spiritual fire with increasing clarity' (ibid.). This also corresponds to Rudolf Steiner's indication—quoted above—that the Group has a direct relationship to the Pauline words and leads to their realization within man. Hence this is a path towards receiving a copy of Christ's Ego.

6. The Sculptural Group and the Modern Mysteries of the Holy Grail

There is, however, much more to be said about the deep mysteries associated with the sculptural Group. For Rudolf Steiner makes a direct connection between the process of receiving copies of Christ's Ego as described in the previous chapter and the Grail mysteries of the present. Thus these are received by people today directly 'at the mere sight of the Holy Grail' (GA 109, 11 April 1909). Hence the sculptural wooden Group is also a way-marker on the path of a person's quest for the Grail. At the beginning of the year 1914, no more than three months after the laying of the foundation stone of the first Goetheanum, Rudolf Steiner spoke the following weighty words in his Grail cycle, *Christ and the Spiritual World. The Search for the Holy Grail*, words which express the inner essence and endeavour of the anthroposophical spiritual stream: 'Let us regard what it is possible for us to cultivate in our anthroposophy as a renewed quest for the Grail' (GA 149, 2 January 1914).

In this cycle Rudolf Steiner describes in particular the circumstances surrounding the quest for the Holy Grail at the time of Parzival. (See GA 149, 1 January 1914.) The path at that time consisted of three stages: a cosmic, a human and a mystical stage. The first stage had to do with observing the sickle of the Moon in the night sky, which cradles the spiritual Sun as in a chalice; the second, human stage resided in an encounter with the virginal mother who holds her dead son in her lap; and the third, mystical stage involved a beholding of the Grail vessel itself.

How can this path to the Grail be followed in the modern mysteries—no longer in the wake of Parzival from the ninth century but in a manner corresponding to the present stage of human evolution? At the end of his life Rudolf Steiner wrote about this modern Grail quest, which is associated today with the new, spiritual-scientific understanding of the Mystery of Golgotha and its consequences, indicating 'that a new and full understanding of the Mystery of Golgotha will unfold in our age out of the consciousness soul in the light of Michael's activity'.[63] For 'the world pictures in which the mysteries of Golgotha were living' form the substance of the Grail chalice in the supersensible worlds (ibid.). And so these three stages of the Grail quest, which Rudolf Steiner describes in the cycle referred to with regard to Parzival, can be characterized in an altogether different way for our time out of anthroposophy.

Consequently, the first, astronomical stage is no longer associated with observation of outward heavenly bodies, as was appropriate for Parzival on his path to the Grail castle. For in our time the decisive step must be taken from an outward to an inner astronomy: 'We must arrive at an astronomy from within, so that the course of the world through the Saturn, Sun, Moon, Earth, Jupiter, Venus and Vulcan periods can be awakened within man out of visionary powers: an astronomy from within where there was formerly an outward astronomy' (GA 202, 23 December 1920). This 'inner astronomy', with a knowledge of Christ at its core, forms the central aspect of the content of *Occult Science*. There it is described as the 'knowledge of the Grail', which represents 'the new initiation knowledge, with the Christ mystery at its centre' (GA 13).

The next stage of the Grail quest reveals the second, 'human aspect of the Holy Grail' (GA 149, 2 January 1914), which at the time of Parzival consisted in the figure of the 'mother with Jesus, with the Christ' (ibid.).[64] This aspect of the Grail mystery is *in our time* included in the sculptural Group. No longer does the Moon mother carry her dead son; but here instead an earthly human being is depicted who has received the cosmic human being into himself and has thereby passed from death to eternal life. We have an archetypal picture of this in the Baptism in the Jordan, when Jesus of Nazareth as *the human Grail* took the spiritual Sun of the world, the living Christ, into his own being. Rudolf Steiner refers to *this* aspect of the Grail in connection with the sculptural Group in the following words: 'This central figure can be called "man", the cosmic human being manifested in an earthly personality, as the Christ was manifested in an earthly personality—in a life lived in historical time—through Jesus of Nazareth' (GA 159, 15 May 1915).

On this basis one can say: if today we approach the sculptural Group in a meditative, contemplative way, we have before us the modern revelation of the Grail mysteries, a spiritual place where the 'knowledge of the Grail'—which was brought to expression in an imaginative form in the first Goetheanum—is as though summarized in the single form of its central figure, so that a person who is standing before it can say: yes, this is indeed the modern Grail. But it is in our time understood and brought to visible expression 'out of the consciousness soul in the light of Michael's activity'. As did the 'Pietà' for Parzival in the ninth century, so does the figure of the Representative of Humanity in the twentieth/twenty-first century and far beyond form the gateway to the true mysteries of the Grail.

As for the third stage of experiencing the Grail, a full description of it would go beyond the limits of the present book. Nevertheless, an essential aspect needs briefly to be discussed here. According to Chrétien de Troyes the Grail is brought into the room of the castle 'like a kind of key', so that 'all lights in the room are outshone by the light of the Holy Grail, as the stars are outshone by Sun and Moon'. This radiance appears today as 'what shines towards us through the light of thought of that dodecahedral Foundation Stone of love which is shaped in accordance with the universe and has been laid into the human realm' (GA 260, 25 December 1923) and which unites the human soul directly with the 'Sun of Christ' that shines at the centre of the Grail mysteries. Thus this Foundation Stone of love of the Christmas Conference forms a secret key to the modern Grail mysteries, as has already been described at some length elsewhere.[65]

Returning to the second stage of the aspect of the sculptural Group that has been described, it should also be pointed out here that what Rudolf Steiner—albeit only with great delicacy—expressed at one point of the lecture during the Christmas Conference on the anniversary of the destruction of the first Goetheanum can be properly understood against this background. After the karmic connection between the Goetheanum and the Temple of Ephesus (356 BC) had been explained, he continued: 'In Ephesus the statue of the Gods; here in the Goetheanum the statue of Man, the statue of the Representative of Mankind, Christ Jesus, through which—*by identifying ourselves with Him*—we thought to attain to knowledge in all humility, even as in their way, a way that is no longer fully understood by mankind today, the pupils of Ephesus formerly attained to knowledge through Diana of Ephesus' (GA 233, 31 December 1923). What does *identifying* ourselves 'in all humility' with the image of the Representative of Humanity mean in this connection? Surely none other than embarking in full consciousness on the path that leads to the experience which is described in the words of St Paul: 'Not I, but Christ in me'. For if someone truly experiences this in his soul, he has at the same time fully identified himself microcosmically with the image of the Representative of Humanity in the same way that, on a macrocosmic plane, it was possible for the first time on Earth for Jesus of Nazareth when he received the Christ at the Baptism in the Jordan.

In this way it becomes possible in the modern Grail mysteries to be the bearer of a copy of Christ's Ego[66] and, hence, a true Christophorus, as is portrayed in the central figure of the sculptural Group.

7. The Mystery of the Etherization of the Blood and the Figure of the Representative of Humanity

A further aspect of the central figure of the Group, a feature which has a particular relationship to the mystery of the copies of Christ's Ego, has to do with the enigmatic forms on the right side of the forehead[67] of the Representative of Humanity and the large wavelike forms on his chest, which well forth from the region of the heart like a whirling stream of etheric forces. If one lets these two movements blend to some extent with one another, what emerges in the form that results from this is a complete connection of the spiritual forces of the heart and the head, as is described in the fourth part of the Foundation Stone Meditation. This is the deeper reason why we can turn to Christ with the plea:

> O Light Divine,[68]
> O Sun of Christ,
> Warm Thou
> Our hearts,
> Enlighten Thou
> Our heads
>
> (GA 260, 25 December 1923).

For already during His life on Earth Christ fully established this harmony between heart and head, that is, between love and wisdom.[69] It was for this reason that He became the greatest model for what from our time onwards must consciously be attained, that is, creating a balance and, hence, a complete reconciliation between the Spirits of Wisdom and the Spirits of Love, which battle with one another in the subconscious minds of human beings. Rudolf Steiner says of this: 'If we penetrate the veil of phenomena, we see ... a divine-spiritual world of activity of a hierarchic nature. And what strikes us initially is the great battle that is taking place behind the scenes of the physical world of the senses between wisdom and love. Man is placed in the middle of this battle. For a long time he was unconscious of it; in future he must engage ever more consciously with this battle that is enacted in the world between wisdom and love. For it should be man that emerges from the ceaseless pendulum swings in the battle between wisdom and love, at times veering towards wisdom and at others towards love ... In those nether regions where unconscious instincts hold sway, the Spirit of Wisdom stands against the Spirit of Love, and the Spirit of Love against the Spirit of Wisdom. But from our age of consciousness-soul evolution onwards, this rises up into our conscious minds. Man must settle this battle within himself' (GA 186, 20 December 1918).

One can find the harmonious merging of these two principles of wisdom and love in the Representative of Humanity. For it is He who in our time gives man the spiritual strength so that the battle between the Spirits of Wisdom and of Love can 'victoriously' be fought out in the human soul (ibid.). These elements are portrayed in the following way in the central figure of the sculptural Group. *Wisdom* can be discerned in the three folds on the forehead of the Representative of Humanity which run in a leftward direction from the root of the nose.[70] And then one observes the mighty, wavelike streams on His chest proceeding from the region of the heart, which as they ascend form, as it were, an arc towards the left from below upwards, to be representative of *love*. Around the heart region, however, the lower streams constitute a distinctive, threefold form which encompasses the heart and then rises up in three streams to the uplifted left hand. These three streams issuing from the heart correspond in a distinctive way to the movement of the three folds on the forehead of the central figure, which can likewise be viewed as three—albeit smaller—streams. A closer, meditative study soon reveals their mutual affinity. Furthermore, they stream towards one another almost as a matter of course and achieve the union of wisdom and love in a mighty, upward flowing form which connects the head and heart of the Representative of Humanity to one another in a threefold way. (See illustration on p. 45.)

This unique form, which clearly has no physical origin but is of an etheric nature,[71] makes the words with which Rudolf Steiner characterizes the essence of Christianity as greater than all religion[72] artistically visible in a work of sculpture: 'First wisdom, then love, then a wisdom warmed through with love' (GA 102, 24 March 1908). Here wisdom corresponds to the three folds on the forehead, love to the threefold form around the heart and the etheric connection between the two threefold streams manifests the 'wisdom warmed through with love', the highest representative of which on Earth is Christ Jesus.[73]

A further step towards understanding this etheric edifice can be taken if one makes a closer study of the countenance of the Representative of Humanity in the central form of the corresponding painting on the small cupola, which Rudolf Steiner personally executed together with the preparatory sketch for it (see pp. 40 and 41). On the right temple of the forehead one can discern a further motif with three folds, which sculpturally bend round from the left at the top down to the right and then flow together as in a point. This second—likewise threefold—etheric stream is then taken up and continued on the right side of the body, so that it extends down to the solar plexus. Thus the first, left or heart stream is the one that imbues wisdom with love (in the sense of Rudolf Steiner's words which have been quoted). The right stream then in the opposite direction fills and permeates love with wisdom. (See the illustrations on pp. 44 and 45.)

The two etheric streams manifestly correspond to the mighty gestures of the hands. Thus the first stream has a strongly angled form, which follows the upward movement of the left hand. The second stream, which flows in the direction of the hand that is extended downwards, indicates a line of direction that is only slightly inclined. Together they form a complete etheric cycle which, in the Representative of Humanity, manifests the archetypal picture of what Rudolf Steiner describes in the lecture on 'The Etherization of the Blood'.[74]

In this lecture Rudolf Steiner speaks of two important streams within man: the microcosmic one that flows from the heart to the head, and the other, macrocosmic one that flows from the cosmos through the head down to the heart. This latter macrocosmic etheric stream flowing from above to below can be discerned quite clearly on the right side of the figure of the Representative of Humanity. 'Two streams can therefore be perceived in man—one deriving from the macrocosm and the other microcosmic in nature' (ibid.). Rudolf Steiner says of this latter stream: 'In the region of the heart there is a continual transformation of the blood into this delicate etheric substance which streams upwards towards the head' (ibid.). This etherization of the blood in the region of the heart is wonderfully depicted on the left side of the chest of the Representative of Humanity. (The threefoldness of the streams is indicative in this sense of the three higher kinds of ether, the light, sound and life ethers.) This stream of the etherized human blood of Jesus of Nazareth was imbued with the Ego of Christ after the Baptism in the Jordan and can therefore be called the stream of the etherized blood of Christ.

Thus one can understand the gestures of the outstretched arms of the Representative of Humanity on this *etheric* plane: with His raised left arm He gives direction to the macrocosmic stream and at the same time guards it from the attacks of Lucifer. And with the gesture of His right arm He ensures that Ahriman has no access to man's middle region, where a delicate process of the etherization of the blood is taking place, so that this can unfold in complete purity and without any influence from without, following its own laws alone.

Pencil study of the countenance of Christ for the painting on the small cupola of the first Goetheanum

Countenance of Christ from the central motif on the small cupola of the first Goetheanum

In an early lecture Rudolf Steiner gives a short description of the human being of the future, in whom three organs in particular will play a central role. 'In times to come there will only be three organs: the heart as a Buddhi organ, the two-petalled lotus-flower between the eyes and the left hand as an organ of movement' (GA 93a, 29 September 1905). Precisely these three places are strongly emphasized in the figure of the Representative of Humanity and together give rise to a particular form which in a prophetic way points already today towards such a future time. This is further confirmed in that in his early lectures Rudolf Steiner on several occasions refers to Christ as the bearer of the cosmic Buddhi principle. (See, for example, GA 96, 1 April 1907.) Thus after Christ's union with Jesus of Nazareth at the Baptism in the Jordan His heart has become such a Buddhi organ, which will develop in future within all human beings.

Everything that has been previously said comes to manifestation with particular clarity in the central figure of the sculptural Group.[75] (See the illustrations on pages 44 and 45.)

The three points of this etheric cycle correspond precisely to the three stages of the structure of the fourth part of the Foundation Stone Meditation. Beginning with the 'Sun of Christ', the hearts of human beings are first addressed, then their heads and finally their will with its aspiration to the good ('that good may become ...'). The etheric movement in the central figure of the sculptural Group unfolds in a directly comparable way. The whole of the etheric stream gathers as though in a great chalice in the region of the heart, then rises up to the head in a wide arc extending in a leftward direction in order—after an inner transformation in the ego point (between the eyebrows)—to begin the downward path (now on the right side) towards the solar plexus, where the wisdom that has been warmed through with love takes hold of the will itself and leads it forward, so that it may do only what is good in the world.[77]

If one follows this cycle in the opposite direction, one returns from the solar plexus to the head and finally to the heart. Cosmologically these three stages signify the aeons of Old Sun,[78] Old Moon and Earth.[79] Thus in the etheric currents of the central figure of the sculptural Group the whole process of the involvement of the Christ Spirit with earthly evolution is portrayed. If, moreover, one bears in mind that the beginning of Christ's direct relationship to the cosmic evolution of the Earth goes back to the time of Old Sun, where He was the leading spirit of this aeon,[80] it becomes understandable that this connection lives primarily in the etheric body (as man's body of memory).[81]

The solar plexus is particularly associated with the etheric body. It is 'the organ of the etheric body' (GA 93a, 7 October 1905). It was incorporated in the physical body by higher beings on Old Sun, so that man could receive his new member, the etheric body. 'The solar plexus also came into being in this solar cycle, an organ which bears the name it does because it is an actual organ of which only rudiments remain today' (ibid.).

Nevertheless, Christ forms a connection with this organ, which is today only in a rudimentary state, in order to live initially only as an etheric being in Jesus of Nazareth immediately after the Baptism in the Jordan.[82] Rudolf Steiner has this to say about this 'etheric' presence of Christ in Jesus, which during the three years of His earthly life was increasingly renounced in order that the God could become man: 'But in the course of the earthly life of three years ... the Christ Being—*as an earthly being*—assumed an ever closer likeness to the physical body of Jesus of Nazareth' (GA 148, 3 October 1913). And somewhat later in the same lecture he adds: 'In the same measure in which this etheric Christ Being identified with the body of Jesus of Nazareth, to that same degree did Christ become man' (ibid.).

On the basis of what has been said it also becomes understandable why, in the figure of the Representative of Humanity, this part of the body is portrayed in a somewhat emphasized way, that is, as a place in man's being where the forces of the macrocosmic stream extending from above downwards are as though taken up by the solar plexus and are thereby held back from penetrating the lower regions of the body.

If one concentrates especially on the mighty swirling form around the heart region of the central figure, one can also discern something else; for here we have to do with the birth of the *new* etheric stream which rises from the heart to the head and which is the stream of the etherized blood of Christ. The two etheric streams already in existence, the macrocosmic one (from the head to the heart[83]) and its microcosmic counterpart (from the heart to the head) were already present within man long before Christ's appearance on the Earth. But what was added through His incarnation was the new etheric stream referred to above. It is the arising of this stream through Christ's presence within Jesus of Nazareth which is (among much else besides) brought to visible expression in the figure of the Representative of Humanity. However, this mighty form in the region of the heart also has additional significance. It represents the initial flowing of this new etheric stream which, since the Mystery of Golgotha—or, to be more precise, after the blood had flowed from the wounds of Christ Jesus and had become united with the Earth—can now be found in each earthly human being.

The figure of the Representative of Humanity

The Mystery of the Etherization of the Blood

The figure of the Representative of Humanity, showing the etheric streams

Rudolf Steiner goes on to speak in the lecture 'The Etherization of the Blood' of the need to unite these two etheric streams—those of man and of Christ—which flow from the heart up to the head with one another in our time. This union comes about today only if a person acquires a knowledge of Christ and His deed on Golgotha that is appropriate for now. Only then do these two streams unite within him. This, too, is portrayed in an archetypal way in the figure of the Representative of Humanity: the two streams in their primordial unity in Jesus of Nazareth, whose blood was imbued with the cosmic Ego of Christ during the three years and had wholly become His blood.

What is manifested in this way in the Representative of Humanity as the union of both streams is at the same time the principal condition that we must fulfil in ourselves in order to achieve a conscious perception of the etheric Christ (ibid.). Hence a meditative study of the central figure of the Group can awaken and strengthen the inner forces within man that lead to an experience of Christ in the etheric.

All this is inseparably connected with the copies of Christ's Ego which await people who are prepared for them in the spiritual world. According to Rudolf Steiner they are kept in the Grail chalice that is present there. (See GA 109, 11 April 1909.) However, human beings can make themselves ready for the receiving of these copies only by uniting wisdom and love at the highest level in complete harmony through an inner development which has Christ as its central focus ('knowledge of the new initiation, with the Christ mystery at the centre'[84]).[85] Only in this way can the foundation be laid for the transition from the Earth to the future Jupiter or from the cosmos of wisdom to the cosmos of love. 'The "cosmos of wisdom" is thus evolving into a *"cosmos of love"*. All that the ego is able to bring to development needs to become *love*. The exalted Sun Being whom it was possible to characterize in describing the evolution of Christ manifests Himself through His revelation as the all-embracing "ideal of love". The seed of love is thereby planted in the innermost core of man's being; and from there it shall stream forth into the whole of evolution' (GA 13, the chapter entitled 'Present and Future Evolution of the World and of Mankind'; italics Rudolf Steiner).

This can be seen from the artistically formed etheric streams of the central figure of the sculptural Group. From there it becomes discernible how the seed of love which has been implanted in every human heart through the Christ event takes hold of the wisdom in the head and then leads in the will to the 'highest imaginable ideal of human evolution', to '*spiritualization*' (ibid.).

Only if in this way the 'all-embracing "ideal of love"' that is depicted in the Representative of Humanity is pursued in freedom is man capable of receiving a copy of Christ's Ego which awaits him in the Grail mysteries of the present, so as to become in this or in a subsequent incarnation a true 'Christophorus'. Rudolf Steiner refers to this relationship in the following words, which have a direct connection with the central figure of the sculptural Group in the sense of what has been described above: 'The copies of the ego of Jesus of Nazareth are waiting for us in the spiritual world for the future evolution of mankind. People who can raise themselves *to the heights of spiritual wisdom and love* are candidates for these copies of the ego of Jesus of Nazareth; and they then become Christ bearers, true Christophori. It is their task on this Earth to prepare for His Second Coming' (GA 109, 31 May 1909).

In the last sentence of this quotation the two most important themes of anthroposophical Christology merge: man's connection with a copy of Christ's Ego—and the reappearance of Christ in the etheric. For both of these the Representative of Humanity stands there as a key figure pointing the way forward.

8. An Encounter with the Representative of Humanity

The motif on the left-hand side of the Group stands in the strongest contrast to the path of the ego represented by the central motif;[86] for it portrays the path to the realm where the adversarial forces exercise dominion—the eighth sphere—and, hence, from the outset is indicative of a clear anti-ego tendency which leads to the cosmic domain of the Asuras.[87]

According to Rudolf Steiner the forces of visionary body-bound clairvoyance are likewise associated with the eighth sphere. (See GA 254, 18 October 1915.) Thus people who admire these qualities and revere those who bear them are inwardly already on the way to the eighth sphere. Rudolf Steiner even speaks in this regard of a 'perverse love' for it. Meditative study of the sculptural Group can work in a contrary direction, in that it is able to create the necessary counterweight in the human soul and therefore protect it from the temptation referred to.

As one looks at this unique work of art for the first time one has the overwhelming sense of a direct encounter with the central figure, which fully takes hold of and fills the observer's soul. From this a further experience can gradually unfold, which may be described as follows. It does, of course, have the strongest potential influence in the course of one's *first* encounter with the original of the wooden sculpture in the Group room of the Goetheanum. However, it can also repeatedly be evoked in a similar way with each further visit through a certain inner meditative attitude.

The Representative of Humanity advances towards us with His mighty gesture in such a way that one initially perceives nothing else around Him; for He alone fills the observer's entire field of vision. One beholds this indescribable countenance, which brings to expression the highest concentration of wonder, compassion and conscience, as though in a state of enchantment. In this moment one can indeed experience what Rudolf Steiner himself says in this regard: 'Christ stands there as the embodiment of love,'[88] which he radiates forth in all directions.

One comes to oneself again only gradually from this deep sense of awe and experiences something akin to an inner urge to follow the two directions indicated by the mighty gestures of the arms and hands. On this path one gradually becomes aware of the surroundings of the Representative of Humanity extending in both an upward and a downward direction. Thus the first thing that one perceives, forming a great arc above the head of Christ, is Lucifer falling into the abyss; his wing is broken in exactly the place where the left hand of the Representative of Humanity almost touches him as it radiates forth. However, the gesture of this left hand has nothing judgemental about it. It is pure love and compassion. But it is just this that Lucifer cannot bear, and he falls into the abyss in order to avoid this encounter.

If one follows the gesture of the right hand, one discovers the figure of Ahriman deeply entrenched in a cleft of the Earth. He lies there with broken, batlike wings and a fossilized, dragon- or wormlike body, bound by veins of gold as he flees from an encounter with the purity of cosmic love and its boundless compassion for all beings of the world. But in this case too it is not that Christ hates him, but rather does Ahriman in his despair drive himself to a state of ultimate solitude. For both adversaries it is the hour of true *self-knowledge*. 'Lucifer feels something within himself that makes him break his own wings. Here Lucifer comes to recognize himself, to experience himself. The same holds true of Ahriman' (GA 157, 10 June 1915).

Because Rudolf Steiner emphasizes in particular Christ's compassion for both adversaries (He has 'infinite compassion' for Lucifer and also 'infinite compassion for Ahriman',[89] it becomes immediately understandable that the whole sculptural Group has a connection with the Parzival impulse. 'Christ, however, stands in the middle [of the sculptural Group] as the one who brings the Parzival element into the modern age and who, *not through His power but through His essential Being*, induces the others [Lucifer and Ahriman] to overcome themselves, so that it is they who do the overcoming rather than being overcome by Him' (GA 159, 18 May 1915). Herein tacitly lies the fundamental difference between the impulse of Parzival and that of Christ. Parzival gains knowledge in his own right through the power of compassion; whereas Christ engenders higher knowledge in other beings through His presence. This arises out of the Christ consciousness which He calls forth within man, a quality which in a deeper sense is associated with all true self-knowledge.[90] For this reason Rudolf Steiner can also speak of the self-knowledge of Lucifer and Ahriman, which became possible for these beings after the Mystery of Golgotha, as is portrayed in the sculptural Group.

Through such an encounter with Christ man likewise awakens to the highest degree of self-knowledge, a process which—albeit in a completely different way—is just as painful for him as for the adversaries. For where Christ is concerned His essential Being works upon a person's soul in such a way that it is not Christ who judges him (as the Christian Churches still believe today, and as Michelangelo painted in an almost archetypal form in his great fresco *The Last Judgement*) but the human individual judges himself in the presence of Christ Himself. And the judgement is then irreversibly true to the extent that this Being is the one who brings this about through His presence alone.

Rudolf Steiner connects this inner process of self-knowledge, which leads to a total self-transformation, with the future of Christianity. While comparing in this sense Michelangelo's picture of Christ in *The Last Judgement* with the central figure of the sculptural Group, he says: '[Michelangelo's] Christ cannot be the Christ of the future, for on the one hand He rewards the good and on the other condemns the evildoers; whereas for Christians of the future what will happen is that they will each reward and condemn themselves because of what has come into the world through Christ' (GA 157, 10 June 1915). This new Christian power of true self-knowledge, which leads one to an objective judgement of oneself in the presence of Christ, has already been artistically embodied for these 'Christians of the future' in the sculptural Group; and an unprejudiced observer can gain a sense of such an influence. This can be developed into a real inner experience through individual contemplation.

The Russian poet and anthroposophist Maximilian Voloshin (1877–1932) referred to this mystery of the future in the following words from the last, fifteenth poem, 'The Judgement', of his great poetic work *The Paths of Cain*:[91]

> And each one
> Glimpsed the sun within himself
> In the zodiac ...
> ... And *judged himself*.[92]

Through a meditative study of the sculptural Group, as has been described here, one can also discover the essential features of the entire methodology of anthroposophy. Above all in recognizing the nature of evil, which according to Rudolf Steiner is one of the central tasks of our time, that of the fifth post-Atlantean epoch, one begins in accordance with this methodology by directing one's inner eye initially towards the good, uniting oneself firmly and unshakeably with it and, only then, firmly standing on this foundation, one turns one's gaze also towards the evil. This basic methodological principle must be consistently applied in the encounter with every human being and in every situation in life, so that it becomes a natural habit within one's soul. Studying the wooden sculpture in an ever renewed way can be distinctly helpful for this.

9. The Cosmic Source of the Forces of Healing

If one intensively and regularly concerns oneself in an active way with the sculptural Group, the further discovery can be made that a meditative engagement with it also reveals to the observer the source of primal healing qualities; for from an anthroposophical point of view most human illnesses arise from illegitimate influences of the adversaries,[93] which disturb the original connection of the human organism as a microcosm with the health-bestowing harmony of the spiritual macrocosm. In contrast to this, a study of the sculptural Group represents a sure path whereby the influences of the adversaries which cause illness are driven out through the Christ impulse being received into man's rhythmic system, while at the same time the primal impulse of healing is awakened within man. According to Rudolf Steiner, the Representative of Humanity represents the picture of the highest human qualities (see page 19) and is therefore associated with the source of all health-bringing forces on Earth and in the cosmos.

The following extract from Rudolf Steiner's writings indicates how such a healing can from our time onwards become possible with ever greater frequency and also happen in a concrete way: ' "Christ gives me my humanity"—that will be the fundamental feeling which will well up in the soul and pervade it.' And indeed, this constitutes the strongest experience which the observer of the central figure can derive from the wooden sculpture. But then Rudolf Steiner immediately adds: 'Once *this* feeling is present, another also comes: man feels himself to be raised by Christ beyond mere earthly existence, he feels at one with the starry surroundings of the Earth and with everything that can be recognized in this starry mantle as spiritual and divine.'[94]

This enables one to understand in what sense Christ becomes the greatest healer of an ever more ailing human nature[95] above all in our fifth post-Atlantean cultural epoch. For because of its close relationship to the physical body and, hence, to the earthly world, the consciousness soul has a strong inner tendency to make people objectively ill, on the grounds that it increasingly separates them from the world of the spiritual cosmos, from the 'starry surroundings' of the Earth. Christ has the task of bridging this abyss between man and the divine-spiritual starry cosmos which must inevitably arise in our epoch; for of all divine beings He alone has descended from the spiritual world to the Earth and lived there for three years in the physical body of a human being, Jesus of Nazareth. In this way

Christ fully brought about in a human life what Rudolf Steiner expressed with regard to the middle figure of the wooden Group, that what was depicted here was 'cosmic man ... expressed in an earthly individual' (GA 159, 15 May 1915).

Such an earthly individual who in this way bears within Himself a relationship to the cosmic world is not only absolutely healthy in Himself but, through being in constant harmony with the spiritual forces of the entire cosmos, becomes to the highest degree a source of healing forces on the Earth. Rudolf Steiner refers to this in his book *The Spiritual Guidance of Man and of Humanity*: 'Christ stood constantly under the influence of the entire cosmos; He took no step without cosmic forces exerting their effect upon Him' (GA 15, ch. III). And how did He carry out His healings? By becoming—in Jesus—a mediator between human beings and the forces of the cosmos: 'Christ Jesus is portrayed [in the Gospels] as the intermediary who brings the sick into connection with the forces of the cosmos, which at precisely that time were able to work in a healing way' (ibid.).

What was at the Turning Point of Time to be perceived more in individual sick people[96] concerns in our time the whole civilized world with its impulses that cause illness. Thus Rudolf Steiner says with respect to our fifth post-Atlantean cultural epoch: 'The ordinary life of people from our fifth post-Atlantean epoch onwards is, therefore, in a sense a gradual process of becoming ill. Accordingly, all education and all cultural influences must be directed towards making people well. In a certain way this is the first true activation of the Christ impulse: healing. This is its special task in the fifth post-Atlantean epoch—to be the Saviour, the One who heals' (GA 186, 7 December 1918). Hence a person's inner connection with the sculptural Group leads today to the source of the healing forces which can above all counteract this all-pervading sickness of modern civilization.

It can be shown by means of an example brought by Rudolf Steiner in what sense the healing forces necessary for present-day humanity can be found in the sculptural Group. In the lecture of 27 May 1910, at the end of the Hamburg cycle entitled *The Manifestations of Karma*, Rudolf Steiner draws back the veil from the great mystery of the outward sense-perceptible world and the human soul. For if one follows the spiritual-scientific path of knowledge in both directions to the end, one arrives at a surprising discovery. One learns that all the material substance of the world is ultimately nothing but congealed light, and the nature of the soul consists of the substance of love. Thus the two words 'light' and 'love' explain the countless mysteries of the outer world of nature and the inner world of the human soul. 'In the sentence: "matter is woven light, and the soul is in a certain sense rarefied love" are to be found the keys of countless mysteries of earthly existence' (GA 120).

Rudolf Steiner then in the same lecture brings this twofold discovery of his spiritual research into connection with the healing process in man, and with the essential nature of the remedy that overcomes illness: 'We either derive the remedy from our surroundings, from condensed light, or from our own soul through a healing deed of love, an act of sacrifice, in which case we heal with the soul power engendered in love' (ibid.).[97] Rudolf Steiner also indicates that a real health of soul and body is to a large extent dependent upon the balance between light and love that exists in a person's nature or can be established ever and again at each moment of earthly life. 'All earthly circumstances are in a sense states of balance between light and love; and everything unhealthy is a disturbance of that balance' (ibid.).

In the next lecture Rudolf Steiner makes these indications more specific by naming the powers which battle, respectively, in nature and in the human soul against light and against love. These are Lucifer and Ahriman. The latter tries to imbue matter with darkness in such a way that man can no longer gain access to its primal condition of light; and Lucifer tries to achieve something similar in the human soul through the pollution of love—as the source of all true soul forces—with desires and passions, above all through egotism of various kinds. (See GA 120, 28 May 1910.)

This result of Rudolf Steiner's research leads us back to the basic motif of the sculptural Group, and we recognize that the balance between Lucifer and Ahriman in the context indicated there also signifies the source of the health which must be created by strengthening the spiritual forces of light within matter and the forces of love within the soul out of the Christ impulse, which is one of balance.

At the end of the lecture, which concludes the cycle referred to, Rudolf Steiner also speaks of Christ's appearance in the etheric and of how through creating balance in the soul not only does a healing of man become possible but also the overcoming of Lucifer and Ahriman (as was later portrayed in the wooden sculpture), in order that, from matter, spiritual light and, from the soul, the purest love for the world and all its beings are able to radiate forth.[98]

10. The Great Decision of Mankind

If one comes to know the sculptural Group in this way it will become an effective means of protection against any influence of the eighth sphere or a 'reaching out of hands' to one another on the part of the adversaries Lucifer and Ahriman, a protective mantle which from our time onwards will be an ever greater necessity for human beings; for already today the demonic enticing power of the eighth sphere, together with its influence on people, is increasing. Rudolf Steiner created this work of art at least in part to set something truly effective over and against this tendency. Nevertheless, as we have seen, it is entirely dependent on the freedom of human beings whether they want to turn towards Christ (principal motif) or towards the eighth sphere (side motif). However, the entire further evolution of the Earth will be determined by what mankind actually decides at this threshold. In this respect a true Parzival question in Christ's name has been posed to people today with the sculptural Group. Hence it is fully justified that—as we have already seen—its central figure is seen as having a close connection with Parzival.[99] If one knows that Parzival was in a previous incarnation Mani, the founder of Manichaeism,[100] who had already prepared the future mysteries of the transformation of evil in his teaching in the third Christian century, one gradually begins to understand how the sculptural Group, with the continuation of its principal motif on the two side-panels of the northern rose-coloured window, is an integral part of the present and future stream of the Manichaean mysteries.[101]

At this point the question must be raised why the third kind of adversaries, namely the Asuras, do not find any direct expression in the wooden sculpture. As already described elsewhere, the path for the Asuras (and even for Sorat) into earthly evolution is opened up whenever man falls prey to the temptation of the *united powers* of Lucifer and Ahriman.[102] For where these two adversaries unite with one another for deeds in common, the balance between them which is the condition for their overcoming can no longer be achieved. In the sculptural Group Christ is depicted as the *Representative of Humanity*, that is, in His connection with the whole evolution of mankind from Saturn to Vulcan—of which the three adversaries likewise form a part. Lucifer remained behind on Old Moon, Ahriman on Old Sun and the Asuras on Old Saturn. The Sun demon (Sorat) does not belong to this evolution; for he is essentially not an opponent of human beings but of Christ Himself and did not have his origin in earthly evolution. Rudolf Steiner says in this connection: 'Sorat is the name of the Sun demon, the opponent of the Lamb' (GA 104, 29 June 1908). In the same lecture Rudolf Steiner also calls him 'an opponent of the Sun', that is, a being who has from the outset battled not only against the Earth as the cosmic place of human evolution but against the Sun as the cosmic dwelling-place of the Christ.[103]

Nevertheless, the consequences of a wrong decision on the part of mankind—with regard to what comes to expression in the sculptural Group through the united forces of Lucifer and Ahriman—lead further into the world of the Asuras and ultimately into the abyss of Sorat. However, this can happen only if mankind makes the wrong choice in the great decision described above. If present-day humanity resolves this vital decision in the right way, that is, as portrayed in the central motif of the sculptural Group, the gateway to the abyss where the Asuras and Sorat lie in wait for human beings will remain closed as far as the human ego is concerned because of Christ's presence within it, and the whole of earthly evolution can be taken forward under the guidance of Christ and the Time Spirit, Michael, who serves Him.

11. Cosmic Communion and the Essential Nature of the First Goetheanum

As has already been mentioned on page 31, the sculptural Group was to have formed the spiritual heart of the first Goetheanum, endowing the building with its innermost significance. This becomes particularly clear if one bears in mind[104] that the first building was fashioned wholly in accordance with the principle of *cosmic communion*.[105] Rudolf Steiner evoked the nature of this principle in the last lecture that he gave in the first Goetheanum on the evening of the fire. He condensed it into a two-verse mantra which he wrote on the blackboard at the end of the lecture. Only a few hours later this blackboard, together with all the forms and colours of the first Goetheanum, became the sacrifice of a catastrophic fire which destroyed the building on New Year's Eve 1922/23. Thus these mantric words are also a significant component of the spiritual Goetheanum, which is henceforth 'a concern of the ethereal expanses wherein dwells the spirit-filled wisdom of the world' (GA 233a, 22 April 1924):

> In Earth-activity draws near to me,
> Given to me in substance-imaged form,
> The heavenly being of the stars:
> In willing I see them transformed with love.
>
> In watery life stream into me,
> Forming me through with power of substance-force,
> The heavenly deeds of the stars:
> In feeling I see them transformed with wisdom'
> (GA 219, 31 December 1922, translation by Dorothy Osmond)

Cosmic communion itself had to do with the transformation of earthly nourishment on the path of modern initiation, which ascends to Imagination, Inspiration and Intuition. The fluid elements are thereby permeated by the sevenfold forces of the planets and the solid elements by the twelvefold forces of the zodiac. Once this has been achieved by a human being, he can experience himself as the enactor of a cosmic ritual, as one who is freely 'celebrating' in the temple of the cosmos, the consequences of which will be the transformation and spiritualization of the entire Earth. Rudolf Steiner describes this future in great, solemn words: 'Surrendering himself to the universal sovereignty of the cosmic existence that surrounds him, he can experience the act of transubstantiation that is enacted through him in the great temple of the cosmos, standing sacrificially within it in a purely spiritual way ... Man's fundamental relationship to the world ascends from knowledge to a world ritual, a cosmic ritual. The initial stage of what needs to happen if anthroposophy is to fulfil its mission in the world is that man's whole relationship to the world must be recognized as being a cosmic ritual' (GA 219, 31 December 1922).

If one considers the architectural conception of the first Goetheanum more closely from this point of view, one will notice that it was constructed precisely in accordance with the two verses of the mantra of cosmic communion, so that the conclusion of the last lecture that Rudolf Steiner gave in this building brought its essential nature to expression in this mantric form. Thus the Great Hall of the Goetheanum with its portrayal of the seven stages of planetary evolution corresponded to the second part of the mantra of cosmic communion, where the whole wisdom of world evolution was to arise anew in man's experience of the world through feeling. The form of the small cupola, in contrast, corresponded to the first part of the mantra. Here there ruled the sublime peace of the starry world, which found expression in the twelve columns. In connection with the twelvefoldness of these forces, man was able to experience the birth of love as a new creative power out of the depths of his will. The figure of Christ in the sculptural Group placed in the east was to appear as the highest representative of these forces to the beholder, as the spiritual Sun amidst the twelve constellations of the zodiac; for only through His sacrifice on Golgotha on Good Friday was the possibility of cosmic communion given to human beings.[106]

This twofold, sevenfold and twelvefold structure of the first building has a direct relationship to the sculptural Group also from another aspect. For the spiritual forces of the seven planets represent through their influence on man above all what Lucifer would constantly hide from his ego consciousness. Ahriman, on the other hand, seeks from the outset to conceal the relationship to the twelvefoldness of the spiritual forces of the zodiac from the human ego. That these two mysteries could now be revealed in the first Goetheanum and artistically brought to expression in forms and colours in the large and small cupolas happened as the actual consequence of Christ's victory in the soul of an initiate over the two adversaries, as he portrayed this in the principal motif of the sculptural Group.[107]

This revelation can also be traced further in the continuation of the path through the sequence of the coloured windows. The two green windows had to do with the conscious encounter of the modern initiate with the luciferic and ahrimanic forces. Once a person has truly understood their nature and their intentions out of the power of Christ within his ego, it becomes apparent to him what the adversaries otherwise keep hidden from him in the cosmos. The mystery of time and space, as brought to manifestation by the spiritual forces of the planets and the zodiac, can now be properly recognized. This is shown by the two blue windows.

This knowledge in the macrocosm is then taken further in connection with man as a microcosm. (One can also say that now, after gaining a new insight into the nature of the northern mysteries, a comparable insight into the southern mysteries follows.) This is once again a revelation of something that Lucifer and Ahriman otherwise want to keep hidden from human beings: the mystery of birth and death, or unborn-ness and immortality, which must now become fully manifest to a person's mature ego-consciousness (the two violet windows). For only if one considers them together do they enable access to be gained to the essential nature of eternity, with which man comes in contact on his path between two incarnations.[108] Lucifer and Ahriman, however, are in opposition to this: the former veils the knowledge of unborn-ness or man's spiritual life before birth, while the latter hides the true knowledge of immortality or man's spiritual life after death. Their common endeavour in this respect is to separate man's ego-consciousness in the spiritual world from an experience of eternity,[109] the path to which is portrayed in the two violet glass windows. (The last two, the rose-coloured windows, will be discussed in what follows.)

If their content is rightly understood it will be seen that all the window motifs point towards the sculptural wooden Group as the spiritual and artistic focal point of the whole building, and also towards that motif which was depicted in the paintings in the small cupola above the Group; while from the western end of the first Goetheanum this twofold manifestation of the Sun of Christ in the east (in painting and sculpture) was beheld by the human being freely celebrating in the temple of the cosmos, and the countenance of this human figure was portrayed in the central part of the great red window opposite the entrance to the Great Hall. This human individual is in a sublime state beyond space and time, inspired by the cosmic beings of the Bull and the Lion, with fully developed organs of perception (lotus-flowers) and the picture of Michael in his heart; and out of his free will he follows the path of modern initiation, thus preparing himself to meet the Risen Christ who approaches him and at the same time to experience all other aspects of His appearance in past, present and future which flow together into a unity in the sculptural Group.

The particular position of Michael in the heart region of the human being signifies that he wants to find his new dwelling place in human souls: 'Michael, who has been striving from the Sun to the Earth for those who perceive the spiritual element in the cosmos, wants henceforth to establish the focal point of his domain in the hearts and souls of earthly human beings. This is to begin in our present age and will represent a guiding of Christianity into a realm of deeper truths, in that a clear and intimate understanding of Christ as a Sun Being is to arise within humanity through Michael, that Sun Spirit who has always ruled over the Intelligence, who can now no longer administer it in the cosmos but wants in future to administer it through the hearts of human beings' (GA 240, 21 August 1924). The first Goetheanum was concerned with just this 'guiding of Christianity into deeper truths' in a purely Michaelic sense, but above all in what was to be brought visibly to expression in it as a revelation of the present Michael inspiration through the sculptural Group.

Rudolf Steiner had, however, referred to this present task of Michael—which consists in bringing the new knowledge of Christ to humanity during his leadership as the Time Spirit—already five years previously. In the epoch of freedom, such a task is possible only if human individuals out of themselves approach Michael in this endeavour, in order to receive the new wisdom about Christ from his hand. Rudolf Steiner says in this regard: 'Since the end of the 1870s [1879] he [Michael] has been engaged—if we but go to meet him—in imparting an understanding of the Christ impulse in the true sense of the word' (GA 194, 23 November 1919). And in what does this Michaelic understanding of Christ in our time consist? Rudolf Steiner answers this question in the following words from the same lecture cycle, which bears the title 'The Mission of Michael': 'You need to realize that the Christ impulse can be understood only if one views it as the impulse of equilibrium between the ahrimanic and luciferic principles' (GA 194, 21 November 1919). And shortly afterwards he concludes the lecture with the words: 'All this is connected with the mission of Michael in relation to those beings of the higher hierarchies with whom he is associated' (ibid.). Thus it is of great significance to know that a direct message of Michael to present-day humanity is connected both with the sculptural Group and also with the same motif in the paintings in the eastern part of the small cupola.

If the new understanding of Christ emanating from Michael—the cosmic conqueror of Lucifer and Ahriman—is granted to human beings in this way, this means none other than a knowledge of Christ 'in the true sense', that is, an experience of Christ as the Representative of Humanity who by way of an example creates the balance between Lucifer and Ahriman and thereby overcomes both adversaries. Rudolf Steiner brought this 'foundation stone' of the new Michaelic Christianity of our time to expression in the sculptural wooden Group as the inner focus of the first Goetheanum and the spiritual source of its power. From an esoteric standpoint the conception of its architecture was to manifest the present collaboration of Michael and Christ, which man today is not only able to acknowledge but also inwardly to experience through his involvement with the being of the first Goetheanum.

Hence one may say: the modern path from Michael to Christ, which is at the same time for present-day humanity *the* path to the spiritual world, as the fundamental mystery of the first Goetheanum lies between the red window in the west and the sculptural Group (and the similar painted motif in the small cupola) in the east. Or in Rudolf Steiner's words: 'The Michael path, which finds its continuation in the Christ path' (GA 194, 23 November 1919). Hence one can, following Hilde Raske, also call the architectural conception of the first Goetheanum a 'Michael-Christ' impulse,[110] precisely in the sense that Rudolf Steiner describes their present collaboration and brings it to expression by means of this dual designation: '*Michael-Christ* will stand in future as the guiding word at the beginning of the path on which man may arrive at his world goal, in a way that is cosmically right, between the luciferic and ahrimanic powers.'[111] These words from 2 November 1924, which Rudolf Steiner wrote at the end of his life in his studies of the Michael mystery, point directly towards the original impulse of the sculptural wooden Group, on whose central figure he continued to work until the last weeks before his death.

And finally the main motifs of the rose-coloured windows in the Great Hall include the two central aspects of the experience of Christ in the present: in the north the encounter with the etheric Christ (His countenance rises up out of the budding and sprouting plant world) and in the south, on the path of modern initiation, with Christ in His capacity from our time onwards as the Lord of Karma.[112]

The first Goetheanum was in this way, as a unified work of art and the artistic summation of the whole of anthroposophy, oriented towards the three aspects of an encounter with the living Christ that have been described. Thus it manifested the most all-encompassing knowledge of anthroposophical Christology in conjunction with the essential nature of cosmic communion, which was to come to a full realization in this building. For the experience of being in it and contemplating its forms and colours could release the forces in the human soul which in themselves already had the capacity for cosmic communion.

12. The Sculptural Group in the Stream of Time

If we consider the sculptural Group not only from a spatial aspect, as is normally the case with a work of sculpture, but try to sense the mysterious stream of inner time that permeates this unique work of mystery art, we will—without encountering any contradiction—also grasp its relationship to the past, present and future of human evolution.

The relationship of the Group to the past will reveal to us the essential being of Christ *at the Turning Point of Time* as He was in a position to withstand the threefold temptation of the adversaries after the Baptism in the Jordan in order to dwell on the Earth for three years in the body of Jesus of Nazareth, but in such a way that He remained in connection at each moment with the entire spiritual cosmos, because 'the spirit of the whole cosmos' was working within Him (GA 15, ch. III).

Its connection with the present brings the Group into the relationship that has already been indicated with the etheric Second Coming and the revelation of Christ in the cycle of the year in the mighty imagination which an initiate can behold every year at Easter time in the spiritual aura of the Earth: 'The Risen Christ, with luciferic powers hovering above and ahrimanic powers under His feet' (GA 229, 7 October 1923). It is the image of Christ which is 'born out of a state of cosmic becoming in the course of the year' and was 'portrayed through painting and sculpture' in the first Goetheanum (ibid.). And what was to come to manifestation in the sculptural Group was a sublime artistic portrayal of Christ as the new Spirit of the Earth (see GA 103, 26 May 1908), as He is manifested to the clairvoyant vision of an initiate every year in the Easter imagination.

The experience of Christ as the *Lord of Karma*, who takes over this new karmic office within earthly evolution in our time, is likewise an aspect of the Group which quite particularly concerns the present age.[113] The connection of the Group with Christ's activity in the ordering of karma arises from the fact that the forms of the first Goetheanum were fashioned in such a way that they conveyed the power to awaken in the soul that immersed itself in them a deep awareness of karma. (The same is also true of the second building.) For the entire Goetheanum was, in its original architectural conception, built for 'an education in karmic vision' (GA 236, 27 April 1924). And the sculptural wooden Group would then—if it had been placed in the position intended for it—have been experienced there by the observer 'as something in which everything that lived in the forms and which could have been said or artistically portrayed in the

Goetheanum is combined in a single whole' (GA 84, 9 April 1923). It arises from this that above all its forms, which were intended to awaken a perception of karma in the visitor, could reach their true coherence and culmination only through the representation of the Lord of Karma in their midst.

The access to this threefold experience of Christ in the present and also to the whole future of earthly evolution lies in the crucial decision that confronts each person in our time and must be taken freely and consciously. The stark alternatives in this decision are brought visibly to expression in the two motifs of the Group (the central and the left-hand one) like a mighty call to the human heart.

And the future? It manifests itself above all where Rudolf Steiner speaks of how Christ in the sculptural Group also appears in the form that He will adopt in the far distant future: in the way that He will lead mankind from the Earth, on which it has concluded its ego-development, to the Spirit Self and, hence, also to the future Jupiter. For the words with which Rudolf Steiner characterizes above all this future aspect of the main figure of the sculptural Group point towards this: 'Christ *appears to me* in His Jupiter glory, in His future magnificence, binding Ahriman in the sub-earthly realm through bonds of light so that he cannot reach man, and overcoming Lucifer so that he cannot lead the human soul astray on his paths' (GA 161, 3 April 1915).

After mankind's great decision as described above, the path into this future will, however, lead to the most strenuous battles with the forces of evil. In order to win this battle the conclusive and no longer dissoluble inner bond of human beings with Christ in the sense of His words 'And lo, I am with you always, until the end of the world' (Matt. 28:20) must first be forged, which can be attained only on the inner path of fulfilling the 'Not I, but Christ in me'. That people should be bearers of a copy of Christ's Ego—that is the high ideal of the future which Rudolf Steiner brought to visible manifestation in an artistically real way in the sculptural wooden Group. 'It must now be possible to make the ego an organ for receiving Christ' (GA 109, 15 February 1909). For only when the individual ego has become such an organ will it be capable of receiving a copy of Christ's Ego, with the result that the bond with Christ becomes truly real and, hence, indissoluble for all future ages.

This also makes it understandable why Christ, in order to grace human beings with a copy of His Ego, must Himself appear as 'Jupiter man', that is, in the glory of the Spirit Self. This happens in accordance with the pedagogical law which indicates that only the next higher member of man's being can and may with justice be used as a means of influencing any particular member—in this case, the Spirit Self exerting an influence on man's ego.[114]

Rudolf Steiner goes on to say in the same lecture how this relates to the development of Christianity itself: 'Christianity likewise has a physical body, an etheric body, an astral body and an ego ... an ego which at the same time can also take the true Christ Being into itself and rise to ever higher levels of existence' (ibid.). But today the time has come when Christianity must reach the still higher, fourth stage through the appearance of spiritual science. 'Christianity has become "*I*"' (ibid.; italics Rudolf Steiner), Rudolf Steiner therefore proclaims. And the creating of the sculptural wooden Group is the visible sign and at the same time the confirmation of this fact.

The first Goetheanum was erected on the Earth for the sake of this unique possibility on the path of cosmic communion of experiencing the present Christ through a perception of the whole building, with the sculptural Group at its focal point.[115] Hence its tragic loss on New Year's Eve 1922/23 was a catastrophe not only for the history of the anthroposophical movement but also for the further evolution of mankind and the Earth, the far-reaching consequences of which one can still barely fathom today but which were turned by Rudolf Steiner into a *new possibility* for goodness through his mighty deed at the Christmas Conference.

13. The First Goetheanum and the Seventh Apocalyptic Seal

As a visible expression of the book *Occult Science—An Outline* (GA 13) and, hence, of the whole 'science of the Grail' described in it, the first Goetheanum also thereby has a particular relationship to the seventh apocalyptic seal, which Rudolf Steiner specially prepared for the Munich Congress in 1907[116] and is devoted to the mysteries of the Holy Grail. It was Assya Turgeniev who was the first to point this out.[117] Thus in the lower part of the seal there is a fully transparent cube, which embodies the ideal principle of space from which all lower forces have been 'expelled'. This is the pure revelation of the 'From the divine we are born' (the letters EDN—Ex Deo Nascimur—on the edge of the seal). *These* soul forces must, however, be gradually overcome or transformed by man through his inner work on himself and be raised to a higher level.

Then there arises from them the 'world spiral' or cosmic Caduceus, which lifts man up from the world of space to that of time.[118] Now he is in a process of cosmic becoming.[119] In order to enter into this process, man must overcome the forces of death in himself so as to attain to higher life. This happens through the connection with Christ in inwardly experiencing the 'In Christo morimur'. The path as a whole finds its conclusion in the realm of the eternal Spirit (the symbol of the dove), to which the modern mysteries of the Grail give access. (Because of this the chalice is portrayed opening downwards.[120] This still higher stage comes to expression in the third Rosicrucian dictum, 'Per Spiritum Sanctum reviviscimus'.

In this way man passes from the realm of time to that of duration or eternity. This transition is confirmed by the image of the rainbow, which is among other things an expression of the new bond between human beings and the spiritual world—now in the sign of the Spirit.[121]

This threefold step (space—time—Spirit) can also be found in the three first parts of the Foundation Stone Meditation[122] and is depicted in the three portal forms of the first Goetheanum: above the west entrance, above the front of the stage and above the position of the sculptural Group. (See the illustrations on p. 70.)

A visitor coming from the outer world of space enters the Goetheanum and walks through the Great Hall, which with its dynamic metamorphic forms and sculptural portrayals of cosmic evolution brings to expression

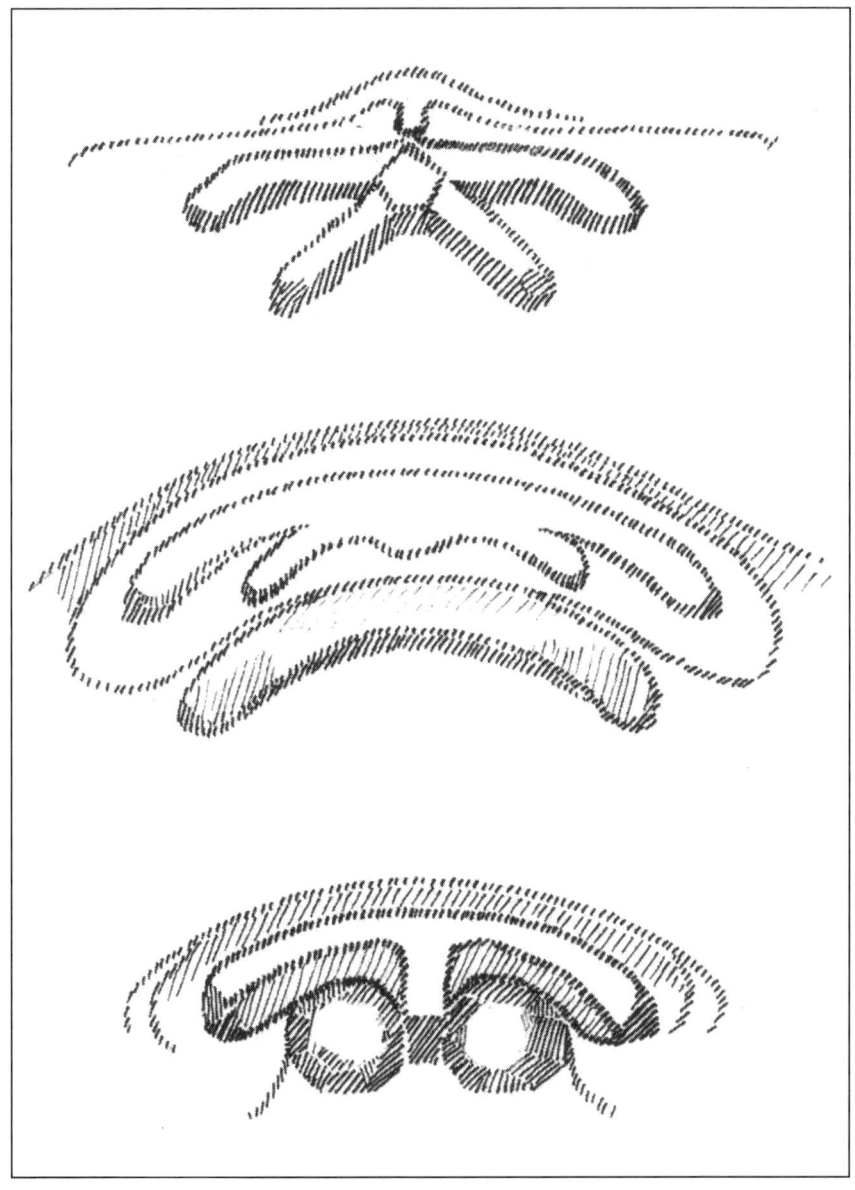

The three portal forms of the first Goetheanum

the process of becoming out of the spiritual nature of time,[123] while the glass windows in the manner of their arrangement like a staff of Mercury[124] indicate to him the way forward. After the opening of the stage curtain his eye is directed towards the future of earthly evolution, where out of the depths of the Grail mysteries the mystery of death is made manifest. This mystery is—among other things—portrayed in the sculptural Group, which, as we have already seen, also brings to expression the essential nature of the third world epoch, that of the Spirit. (See p. 5.)

It is also possible to discern a further connection between the composition of the seventh seal and the sculptural Group together with the same motif in the paintings in the small cupola. Thus the two intertwining snakes in the lower part of the seal correspond to the motif on the left side of the Group. There now follows the transformation of the snakes. A form reminiscent of the staff of Mercury rises up from them such that the observer inwardly creates the staff out of the strength of his own ego and then experiences it as the inner guide leading to the destination where the opposing powers must finally leave the soul. Then out of the inspiration of the Spirit, engirdled by the rainbow, the substance of the Holy Grail becomes perceptible, appearing to the observer in the figure of the Representative of Humanity. Thus one can sense that the central figure of the Group is likewise surrounded by an—invisible—rainbow of colours corresponding to the revelation of the new Isis, which Rudolf Steiner also brings into a connection with the wooden sculpture. (See further regarding the legend of the new Isis in this book.) Rudolf Steiner says of this present Isis-Sophia: 'This Isis is spread out, in her true form, in the beauty of the whole universe, shining towards us out of the cosmos in an aura of manifold radiant colours. We must learn to understand her when we look out into the cosmos and view this cosmos in its aura of radiant colours' (GA 202, 24 December 1920). And the rainbow, which on the seventh seal is surrounded by shining stars, appears to us on the Earth like an earthly reflection of the beauty of the radiant cosmos with its aura of colours. (See the illustration on p. 72.)[125]

Returning to the sculptural Group as the modern revelation of the working of the living Spirit, which appears on the seventh seal in the image of the dove, one similarly finds above the Group, in the eastern part of the building, the form of a chalice, which also closes the seal off from above. Thus we see here, in connection with a pentagon (the motif on the portal arc above the sculptural Group) which is linked through the upward-pointing gesture of its tip with the higher worlds, the form of a double chalice opening in a downwards direction.[126] And below it,

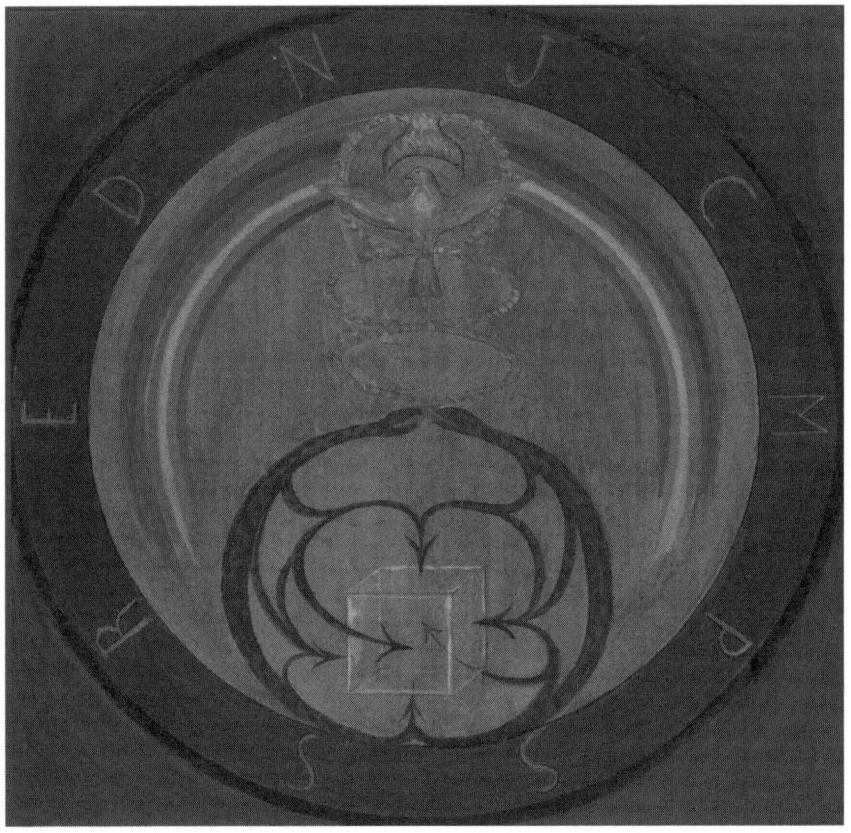

directly above the position of the wooden Group, we find a carved 'baldachin' (canopy)—in which all the forms surrounding it are again united as in a kind of summation—in the form of a chalice again opening downwards (inverted), whose substance was to have been manifested as the great sculpture standing beneath it. (See the illustration on p. 74.) Thus in the seventh seal—albeit as yet only in a germinal form—the whole original architectural conception of the first Goetheanum was anticipated.[127] This shows us with what inner consistency Rudolf Steiner transferred and carried forward the anthroposophical artistic impulse from the Munich Congress of 1907 to the year 1914, in that seven years later he brought the building and the sculptural wooden Group as its spiritual focal point fully to manifestation.

The First Goetheanum and the Seventh Apocalyptic Seal

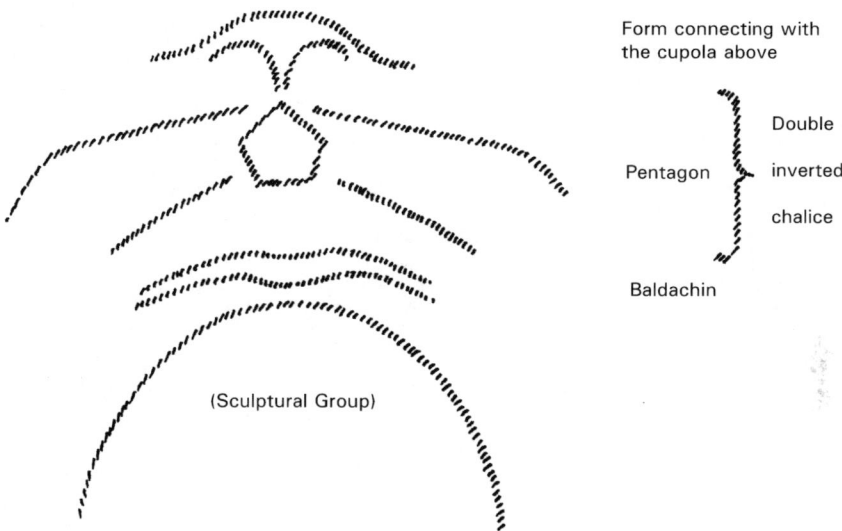

A graphic summary of the portal forms above the sculptural Group in the first Goetheanum

See the illustration on p. 74.

View of the small cupola of the first Goetheanum. The position for the sculptural Group in the centre.

14. The Sculptural Group and the Legend of the New Isis

A further and even more mysterious aspect of the sculptural Group, one that leads wholly into the esoteric domain, will be considered in this chapter. Rudolf Steiner speaks of it in the lecture of 6 January 1918 in connection with the legend of the new Isis (GA 180). He begins his description of it with an unequivocal reference to the first Goetheanum and the sculptural Group: 'It was in the age of scientific profundity, in the midst of the land of the Philistines. Upon a hill in spiritual seclusion was erected a building which was considered very remarkable in this Philistine land ... A statue was intended to be the central point of the building. This statue represented a group of beings: the Representative of Humanity, and a luciferic and an ahrimanic figure.' He goes on to say that 'this statue was actually only the veil for an invisible statue. But people did not notice the invisible statue; for this invisible statue was the new Isis, the Isis of a new age' (ibid.). He emphasizes that it would be entirely wrong to say that the sculptural Group 'signified Isis', because by putting it in such an abstract way something with a purely artistic intention would be completely destroyed, 'for an artistic creation does not merely signify something but *is* something'. In this sense he goes on to describe the spiritual reality as it were behind the forms of the sculptural Group that remains hidden to outward perception: 'And behind the forms was not an abstract new Isis but an actual, real new Isis' (ibid.), and she was as though asleep. Thus the being in question here was a 'sleeping new Isis', but the words that were used to describe her were: 'I am man. I am the past, the present and the future. Every mortal should lift my veil' (ibid.).[128]

The legend goes on to describe the significance of this lifting of the veil of the sleeping new Isis—which every person should accomplish in our time—where it speaks of the awakening or further development of the new Isis, which consists of three stages. At the first she conceives an offspring and gives birth to a being who is the new Horus. As was Osiris in his time this being is dismembered, which, however, applies only to the false, distorted form in which it appears. At the second stage something wonderful then happens: 'There came a day when she could receive her offspring again in its true, in its genuine form from a group of spirits who were elemental spirits of nature; she could receive it back from elemental nature spirits' (ibid.). And if in the sense of what is further related one raises the question as to which elemental spirits could most likely have brought this about, one thinks almost involuntarily of those who are evoked in the three first parts of the Foundation Stone Meditation:

> The elemental spirits hear it
> In East, West, North, South.
> May human beings hear it!
>
> (GA 260, 25 December 1923).

For what do the elemental spirits hear in the Foundation Stone Meditation? It is the essence of the threefold Rosicrucian dictum which tells of the birth, death and Resurrection of Christ Jesus. This is what human beings must now hear! And this, too, is what the new Isis inwardly hears. Hence she can receive her offspring anew from these nature spirits in a true, transmuted form.

When the new Isis had in so wonderful a way acquired her offspring, the power of the new clairvoyance arose within her out of her bond with it. Through this she was enabled to receive a crown, which was initially merely of paper, from a being whom Rudolf Steiner furnishes with the name of 'Mercury'; and equipped with this clairvoyance she came one day—and this was the third and final stage of her development—to what is described in St John's Gospel in order to learn the significance of the Mystery of Golgotha. This enabled the paper crown on her head to be transformed into a shining gold crown of genuine wisdom (GA 180, 6 January 1918).

Thus from this legend of the new Isis in its connection with the first Goetheanum and above all with its focal point, the sculptural Group, it becomes apparent to what a profound degree this building was like a rebirth of the mystery centre of Ephesus in Christian times, where the mysteries of the Word or the Logos had been cultivated before the Turning Point of Time. For in these Ephesian mysteries there still lived the forces of the transition and the harmonious synthesis between the old Egyptian mystery wisdom and the emerging mystery nature of Greece. Moreover, it becomes possible to understand the Goetheanum's designation as the 'House of the Word' through its relationship to the Logos message of St John's Gospel in its full depth and significance; for as the conclusion of the legend of the new Isis indicates, the first Goetheanum (originally also called the *Johannesbau* or Johannes building) was built out of the power of the 'Logos, as lived by Christ here on Earth and among human beings'[129] and as portrayed as the Representative of Humanity in the sculptural Group.

This legend subsequently had a remarkable continuation; for three years later, without any direct reference to his first description of it, Rudolf Steiner gave further explanations—likewise in the Goetheanum—of this legend of the new Isis in the Christmas lectures of 1920. On this occasion he focused no longer on the 'human' aspect of the new Isis but on her cosmic destiny in connection with the divine Sophia, in which human beings were again to play a decisive part. This had to do with the killing of Isis at the threshold of the modern age, that is, at the dawn of the consciousness-soul epoch. Lucifer scattered her and her dismembered body over the visible cosmos. In this way it happened that the cosmos came to be perceived by modern science merely as an ahrimanic picture of purely mechanical laws and was therefore investigated solely in accordance with measure, number and weight.

It is out of this picture that Rudolf Steiner formulates the task of present-day humanity in this second 'legend of the new Isis'. By taking the Christ impulse into their hearts, as described in the first Isis legend, and also by developing new clairvoyant powers, they must undertake the quest for the killed Isis so as to find her with the help of spiritual science and bring her back to life. Rudolf Steiner describes this whole process as follows: 'Oh, this soul [of modern man] will be able to arrive at altogether new feelings if it undertakes to experience the legend of the new Isis in the context of people today: this Isis legend about the killing of Isis by Lucifer and her removal to the cosmic expanses, which have become a mathematical abstraction, that is, the grave of Isis, and then the quest for this same Isis and her discovery through the impulse given by the inner forces of spiritual knowledge, which put in the place of the lifeless sky that which stars and planets are enabled through this inner activity to manifest as monuments of the spiritual powers that surge through space' (GA 202, 24 December 1920).

Moreover, not only must the visible cosmos be perceived in its spiritual foundations through the finding and re-enlivening of Isis but the path towards internalizing the entire cosmos within the human soul also needs to be found on the basis of this knowledge. In other words, man must come to an experience of it not only in space but also in the stream of time. Here the same task confronts us in connection with the legend of the new Isis as has already been described above with respect to the 'science of the Grail' and which Rudolf Steiner formulates as follows in connection with the new Isis: 'We must have a living picture in our minds of all that we have acquired through the newly found Isis, so that the whole heavenly world becomes for us imbued with spirit. We must *gain an inner understanding* of Saturn, Sun, Moon, Earth, Jupiter, Venus and

Vulcan ... We must realize that through the power of Christ [in the first Isis legend through the power of a Johannine understanding of the Mystery of Golgotha] *we need to find an inner astronomy* which reveals the universe to us once more as originating and grounded in the power of the spirit' (ibid.). And if this takes place within man, 'the newly found power of Isis' acquired through 'this insight into the universe' becomes 'the power of the divine Sophia', through which 'the Christ, who has been united with Earth existence since the Mystery of Golgotha' can 'become active within man through being truly known' (ibid.). For in our time it is the divine Sophia herself who through anthroposophy imparts the new knowledge of Christ to earthly human beings, the Sophian knowledge which became visible also to outward perception in the forms and colours of the first Goetheanum. That is, if a person today is truly able to follow the path which in the book *Occult Science* (GA 13) is described as the 'science of the Grail', he will also experience the first Goetheanum in such a way that he is led in it from the new Isis-Sophia to the present Christ.

For the principal task of the first Goetheanum lay precisely in bringing to visible manifestation in the Great Hall how 'the spiritual powers' exert their influence through the seven stages of the planetary evolution of the Earth, and the hierarchies fashion and sustain the entire cosmos in accordance with the spirit through the twelvefoldness of the zodiac. Twelve thrones were made for the hierarchies at the foot of the twelve columns of the small cupola space which were not to be used by human beings of any description.[130] They were put there for sublime beings who were immersed in the contemplation of the spiritual Sun, which has its reflection in the central figure of the sculptural Group. As the renewed twelve initiators of the eternal cosmic mysteries which together encompass the wisdom (Sophia) of the world, they were intended to indicate to human beings of the present an approach appropriate for today to the central Being of the entire cosmos, the Christ.[131]

In this sense the first Goetheanum as a unified work of art represented a path on which the killed Isis was to be found and awakened to new life, so that she would be a legitimate guide to Christ for human beings. And only after a person had through the forms and colours of the first building imbibed and enlivened the power of the new Isis, whom Rudolf Steiner also calls the holy Sophia, would he be enabled to encounter the figure of the Representative of Humanity in the centre of the building and to recognize in Him the etheric Christ. 'Just as the Egyptians looked from Osiris to Isis, so must we learn to look again to the new Isis, the holy Sophia. The Christ will appear again in spiritual form in the course of the twentieth century not through something entering in from without but through people finding that power which is represented by the holy Sophia' (24 December 1920).

As is described in the first new legend, when a person indeed discovers Isis behind the sculptural Group (which corresponds to her veil) he will be making his human contribution to what is objectively wending its way through the world today in the form of the etheric Second Coming. He will then be in a position to behold the Representative of Humanity in a wholly new way, in the light of the newly found Isis–Sophia and so to speak with her eyes, and to recognize in Him the etheric Christ of the present.[132]

15. The Sculptural Group and the Being Anthroposophia

Almost three years later, after Rudolf Steiner had also entrusted the second version of the legend of the new Isis to his pupils, he referred to this path from another aspect on the occasion of the founding of the Anthroposophical Society of Holland in November 1923. At the end of the founding meeting he spoke about the living being of anthroposophy and about how every anthroposophist should receive this being into his heart. For Rudolf Steiner this meant that one experiences anthroposophy as the 'living cosmic being' who 'knocks at the portal of our heart ... and says: Let me in, for I am your true human essence!'[133] And then he added: 'If we allow anthroposophy into our hearts once it has knocked, it brings us by virtue of what it is in itself true *human love*' (ibid.). And if in this way a purely spiritual love is kindled in the soul, a human individual will recognize himself in the central image of the wooden Group: 'Christ stands there as the embodiment of love.'[134]

Thus human love as the free cognitive power of the heart will stream towards Christ as the bringer of universal love. A person standing before the Representative of Humanity will then discover in this unique work of art the most important element in the whole of earthly evolution and, as a consequence of his deepest personal experience, recognize the *central* fact of his soul-life out of the faculties of his own heart: 'The event of Golgotha is a free cosmic deed which springs from universal love and can be understood only through the love in man' (GA 26, Leading Thought 143).

Ten years previously at the first annual general meeting of the Anthroposophical Society (now independent of the Theosophical Society) Rudolf Steiner had already given expression to this theme of self-knowledge, which has so direct a connection with the being Anthroposophia: 'For this is the essence of anthroposophy, that its own being consists of what man's being consists; and the essential quality of its influence is that a person receives through anthroposophy what he himself is and must place this before him, because he must practise self-knowledge.'[135]

And what must an individual place before him as what he has received from anthroposophy? Among many other things that can present themselves to him there is most strikingly its heart, which finds its expression in the sculptural Group; for it is also inseparably connected with the modern path of self-knowledge. Rudolf Steiner speaks about this as follows: 'Thus the "know thou thyself" should as it were sculpturally ring forth through the auditorium, not in abstract forms but moulded in that triune aspect of which I have often spoken and which according to my conviction is the triune quality of future human culture.[136] Hence this wooden figure had to be placed not in the centre of the building but as its focal point.'[137]

Rudolf Steiner also spoke at the Christmas Conference about both these things—the being Anthroposophia and the need for self-knowledge[138]—and as a contemporary way of expressing them used the words: 'Soul of man, know thou thyself in the weaving existence of spirit, soul and body' (GA 260, 25 December 1923). Here too the connection with the central motif of the sculptural Group is very clear; for what matters today is that human beings 'have not abstract matter [Ahriman] and abstract spirit [Lucifer] but an interweaving of spirit, soul and body. *This will be a Michael culture*' (GA 194, 30 November 1919).

Thus the power of Christ as manifested in the wooden sculpture will bring about this harmonious 'interweaving' of spirit, soul and body out of the innermost core of the soul where earthly man's ego-being has its origin, as a sign that a human individual on the path of anthroposophical self-knowledge has come to embody the essential nature of this work of art as an inner foundation for a future Michael culture.

The observations about Rudolf Steiner's wooden sculpture which have been presented in this book may be concluded with some words of his that refer both to the essential nature of the first Goetheanum and to the sculptural Group in its midst and, moreover, derive from a time when no one around him would have any inkling of either of these. Before *the whole of anthroposophy* was placed before humanity in an imaginative way with the first Goetheanum as a unified work of art,[139] in order thereby to indicate with full clarity what constitutes the central focus of anthroposophy as a modern Grail science and was executed in wood and colour (in the cupola paintings) in the figure of the Representative of Humanity, Rudolf Steiner had in the cycle on the Gospel of St John already summarized in the following way in 1909 what has merely been indicated in the present book: 'Thus the anthroposophical world conception views the Christ Being as a kind of focal point in the whole panorama of reincarnation, the being of man, the study of the cosmos and so forth. And whoever gives the anthroposophical world conception proper consideration will say to himself: I can study all of this but I can understand it only when the whole picture converges at the great focal point, the

Christ. I have depicted in a variety of ways the study of reincarnation, of the various human races, of planetary evolution and so on, but I have painted the Being of Christ from a single viewpoint, and this sheds light on everything else.[140] It is a picture with a central figure to which everything else is related, and I can fathom the significance and expression of the other figures only if I understand the main figure.'[141]

And just as in the first Goetheanum the whole of anthroposophy was made visible in an artistic way in order to awaken a new spiritual consciousness in human beings, so does the sculptural Group—which was to form the spiritual focus of the building—not only express the most important knowledge of our Michael epoch but represents the present Michaelic path to Christ which all people today are able to follow.

★

It says in the Old Testament: 'Wisdom has built her house; she has hewn out her seven pillars' (Proverbs 9:1). In pre-Christian times this house of the Sophia was still in the spiritual world and was the place where initiates gained access to the primal revelation of mankind, to the primordial wisdom which was given to human beings when they were driven out of paradise for their path to the physical world of the senses. The divine wisdom or heavenly Sophia had established this spiritual place as an invisible temple out of the forces of the divine Father.

Since the appearance of Christ on the Earth everything secret and concealed had gradually to become manifest there and—in the sense of Goethe's *Fairy Tale of the Green Snake and the Beautiful Lily*—the invisible temple of wisdom had now also to be made visible to all people, though now not out of the forces of the Father but out of those of the Son, who in Christ became man and dwelt amongst men for three years. But in order that this spiritual temple could become accessible to all human beings, the heavenly Sophia also underwent a decisive transformation. (See chapter 14.) She became Anthropos-Sophia (Anthroposophia), in order as such to establish her house or her temple *on the Earth*. This is what happened with the building of the first Goetheanum; it was there that, through Rudolf Steiner, Anthroposophia built herself her house on the Earth.

Moreover, the seven columns of the original spiritual temple of the Sophia, representing the whole evolution of the world from Old Saturn to the future Vulcan,[142] appeared again in the first Goetheanum. Thus in it the house for Anthroposophia was built as a unified work of art in which a human individual was enabled to encounter Christ as the Representative of all Humanity.

Thus the first Goetheanum was the one and only place on Earth in which Christ could reveal Himself in His present etheric form for the first time in the history of mankind. And even after the destruction of the building by opponents of the spirit, the etheric Christ continues to be active in the spiritual Goetheanum, which can be found wherever human beings are working honestly and selflessly for anthroposophy.

Three Supplements

I *The Sculptural Group and the Three Egos of Man*

Rudolf Steiner dealt fully with the mystery of man's threefold ego for the first time in his book *The Threshold of the Spiritual World*.[143] Here it was brought clearly to expression that the ego-organization consists of the earthly ego, the other or higher ego and the true ego, which belong respectively to the three regions of the cosmic whole: the earthly world, the spiritual world and the super-spiritual world (GA 17).

This book appeared in 1913 on the occasion of the first performance of the fourth Mystery Play *The Souls' Awakening* (GA 14), where it was shown how only two of the protagonists are allowed consciously to experience cosmic midnight out of the power of the true ego, Benedictus and Maria. Two years earlier, however, in his well-known Bologna lecture given at the Fourth International Philosophy Congress, Rudolf Steiner had already referred to these three egos; and at the heart of his analysis he focuses upon the relationship of the higher ego to the earthly ego in the sense of a being and its reflection in the bodily sheath.[144]

The experience of the three egos is here also linked with the stages of higher knowledge. Thus if one is to be able to have a direct experience of the reflective character of the earthly ego it is first necessary to achieve a liberation from the physical body, which in spiritual science is called the stage of imaginative knowledge; and in order to proceed to an experience of the higher ego one must rise to the next, inspirative stage, where one lives consciously in one's higher self.

If by following the modern path of schooling one then seeks the transition from Inspiration to Intuition, all the experiences of the higher ego that have been gained will have to be voluntarily extinguished for this step, thus making conscious access to the true ego possible. Rudolf Steiner describes this extinguishing process in the following words: 'Even though inspired knowledge establishes in this way a direct relationship of the self to the supersensible world, the pure beholding of this relationship can be taken still further. This happens through the energetic suppressing of the insight into the self that has been attained ... In the cognitive process characterized here [Intuition] the self is completely excluded.'

In this way a human individual is confronted by the need to make a kind of leap across the cosmic abyss in order to receive his true ego as an act of grace on the part of the higher worlds on the other side. In the cycle

The Secrets of the Threshold, which Rudolf Steiner gave in Munich at the time of the first performances of the fourth Mystery Play, he describes this experience as follows (probably from his own experience): 'But it is quite another matter ... to dwell for a while in the spiritual world at the abyss of existence in confronting nothingness as nothing. It is the most shattering experience that one can have, and one must pass through this experience with great trustfulness. In order as nothingness to traverse the abyss it is necessary that one has the trust that the true ego is brought to meet one from the world. And this is what happens ... Thus the ascent to the super-spiritual world is an inner experience, the experience of a completely new world at the abyss of existence and the receiving of the true ego from this super-spiritual world at the abyss of existence' (GA 147, 30 August 1913). If the question now arises here from which being this grace-filled endowment with the true ego beyond the cosmic abyss is enacted, the answer can only be that the Christ Being is alone capable of this.[145] Rudolf Steiner writes in another context in this sense about man's leap across the cosmic abyss and adds: 'Only through Michael's activity and the Christ impulse can man achieve this leap across the gulf of non-being in relation to the cosmos' (GA 26, Leading Thought 164).

And if in the Bologna lecture this relationship to the true ego is associated with the World Ego, this is a reference to the Ego of Christ, which Rudolf Steiner on numerous occasions and in various contexts calls the World Ego (for example, in the second part of the Foundation Stone Meditation).

Furthermore, the relationship to Christ here becomes even clearer if one supplements the actual content of the Bologna lecture with some thoughts from the written summary of essential points which enabled Rudolf Steiner to add something to his oral explanations. In the lecture itself we find the following remark with respect to the aim of the path of schooling described there: 'And spiritual research could then be thought of as the path of immersing oneself into the essential nature of what is being reflected.' This is a reference to the path that leads from the earthly to the higher ego and beyond to the true ego. In the aforesaid commentary on the lecture, which bears the title 'Theosophy and Modern Cultural Life', Rudolf Steiner refers to the Christological foundations of this path: 'The highest summit of supersensible observation consists in recognizing Christ as the sovereign power in the spiritual world.' And then come these decisive words: 'The more the soul develops supersensible powers of cognition, the closer does it come to the Christ Being.' From this it clearly follows that the more we approach the true ego on the path described, so much the more do we unite ourselves inwardly with the Christ Being. And at the stage of the true ego we receive this Being fully into ourselves.

In the Bologna lecture itself Rudolf Steiner shows how the realms to which the earthly ego and the higher ego originally belong are at opposite poles to one another. For the earthly ego is linked through the senses of the physical body with the entire physical, sense-perceptible world, which is why in ordinary consciousness it feels itself as belonging wholly to this world. The higher ego, in contrast, which does not incarnate in the body when a person is born on the Earth[146] and gives rise only to a reflection of its being in man's physical sheath, is just as closely connected with the spiritual world as the earthly ego is with the physical. And because the higher ego bears in itself the fruits of all incarnations, it can be regarded as that member of man's being which links them all into a higher unity, which one usually terms a person's web of destiny. In Christian terminology one refers to the earthly ego as the personality and the higher ego as the individuality.

Thus in life the earthly ego and the higher ego are as polar opposite as the physical and spiritual worlds. They cannot come together out of themselves, for they do not possess the power necessary for this. Such a power must derive from a still higher Being who—although this is not expressly stated in the Bologna lecture—can only be man's true ego as grasped in Intuition. In the lecture itself, therefore, the stage of Intuition attained on the path of schooling is mentioned at the corresponding place as that authoritative element which brings about the connection between the earthly and spiritual worlds, which in man signifies the union of the earthly ego with the higher ego out of the forces of the true ego.

Hence according to Rudolf Steiner this amounts to 'the synthesis of the sensible and supersensible' and the actual 'converging of the two streams'. However, this only happens at the highest stage of Intuition, which makes possible the connection with the true ego in the act of spiritual communion. 'The converging of the two streams [the sensible and the supersensible] can be thought of as brought about through a possible further development of the life of the soul to the intuitive knowledge that has been characterized. Only within *this* does the possibility arise of overcoming the polarity [of spirit and matter]' (italics Rudolf Steiner).

That this is possible today on the path of modern initiation (the 'further development of the life of the soul') we owe to the events of the Turning Point of Time. At that time there appeared in the Luke Jesus child, whose essential being entered the stream of incarnations for the first time since the Fall, something akin to an archetypal picture of the earthly ego, in which was manifested a pure reflection of the outer world with which the soul of Jesus sought a connection solely through its boundless love and its compassion for all beings. In the twelfth year of this Jesus the ego of the other, Solomon child united with him (this being the ego of the great initiate Zarathustra and did of course involve his higher ego, which was alone capable of such a deed). Thus for 18 years the earthly ego of Jesus and the higher ego of a different being worked together in the bodily sheath of Jesus of Nazareth.[147] Immediately before the Baptism in the Jordan the Zarathustra ego left Jesus of Nazareth and passed into the spiritual world. For the first time in the history of mankind the World Ego of Christ thereupon descended into an earthly human being as his true ego; and through its connection with the true ego the earthly ego or the earth-bound personality was endowed with the character of immortality, which formerly only the higher ego or the individuality of man had possessed.

Through the mediation of the true ego a completely new bond has since then existed between the earthly ego and the higher ego as a foundation of modern initiation. And in the sense of the Bologna lecture a new relationship between the earthly world and the spiritual world thereby becomes possible, thus establishing the foundation for what Rudolf Steiner refers to in his book *An Outline of Occult Science* as the highest aim of earthly evolution, namely the spiritualization of man and the Earth right into physical substances such as emanates from the mature power of a person's ego. 'We see then that the "knowledge of the Grail" culminates in the highest imaginable ideal of human evolution—the ideal of spiritualization, brought about by man's own efforts' (GA 13).

The earthly ego, however, is through its connection with the body and, hence, with the entire physical world of the senses in constant danger of succumbing to the temptation of Ahriman, in that the latter puts the idea into man's head that the physical world accessible through the impressions of the senses is the only reality. In this way he would encourage man to believe that the earthly ego, which is in itself only a reflection (and acquires being only on the basis of its connection with the true ego), represents man's essential nature. Herein lies the classical error of materialism, which would regard man's ego as merely a product of his physical body; for in the materialistic world view the reflection is, purely and simply, considered to be the mirroring being itself.

From this it also becomes understandable why in modern civilization Ahriman battles so vehemently against the general acceptance of the idea of repeated earthly lives and, hence, seeks above all to prevent true knowledge of karma from entering general currency. For his intention is that man should have no access to the higher ego, where all knowledge about previous earthly lives resides. And yet without a connection with his higher ego man becomes a purely earthly being who at some point must also abide by the destiny of the Earth and of his physical body, that is, the prevailing law of death.

The intentions of Lucifer in this regard are altogether different. He does indeed want to lead man to the higher ego but in such a way that the clear consciousness that man has achieved in his earthly ego is completely lost. Consequently he makes the ascent into the spiritual world but—without securing any support in ego-consciousness—enters there into a state of ecstasy which many Eastern philosophers regard quite simply as the highest aim of initiation, and which may be expressed in the image of a drop of light that dissolves in the ocean of divine light. So this is an ecstatic path which can indeed lead one to the spiritual world but only in a luciferic way; and the loss of all earthly memories places one in danger of reaching Lucifer's kingdom instead of that of the good Gods.

Thus mankind stands today in this fateful trial between the working of Ahriman in the West and Lucifer in the East, who do not want to countenance any connection on a spiritual plane between the earthly ego and the higher ego in man. The polarity between Western materialism and a one-sided Eastern spirituality estranged from the Earth comes to manifestation here. This is, moreover, also the context for all the problems existing between the civilization and mentality of the West and the East together with their irreconcilable differences ('clash of civilizations').[148]

The solution to the world problems indicated here—both in human evolution and within the individual human being—can be found only through a real relationship with the Christ impulse and with the true ego that is associated with it. For—in the sense of the Bologna lecture—only this ego is capable of bridging the gulf between the world polarity indicated here and of bringing about a higher harmony. Human evolution, which is otherwise threatened by endless divisions, inexorable military conflicts and other social consequences, will then also go forward in a positive way.

The connection with the sculptural Group is clearly evident from what has been said here. At its focal point there appears the Being who, as the Representative of Humanity, brings to manifestation the highest aspect of the human ego. This Being is the representative of the true ego on the Earth and, hence, has an affinity with every human being. When the true ego shines forth in a human individual, Lucifer can no longer tempt the higher ego from above nor Ahriman the earthly ego from below; for the higher ego acquires through this the necessary connection to the Earth, and the earthly ego enters into a corresponding relationship with the spiritual world. Thus the synthesis of earthly ego and higher ego—and, hence, of Earth and heaven—is attained through the true ego, leaving no further place for the adversarial powers.

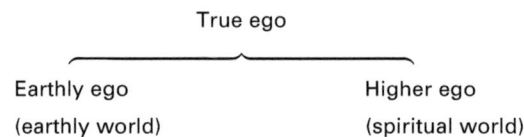

| Earthly ego | Higher ego |
| (earthly world) | (spiritual world) |

In Christian terminology this achievement signifies the acquiring of immortal status by the human personality, which is led by the Christ impulse into a right relationship with the higher ego and, hence, with a person's immortal individuality, which brings all his incarnations together in the spiritual world. Rudolf Steiner expresses this in the following words: 'This is the step forward achieved through Christianity, that the personality is lifted up into the realm of the eternal' (GA 264). And in another context he adds: 'All that man can bring as fruit from a single personality into the individuality he achieves through having a connection with the Christ Being' (GA 102, 24 March 1908).

The artistic expression of this new possibility, which constitutes the entire future of human evolution, is given in the sculptural Group.

II The Sculptural Group and the Redemption of the Adversarial Powers

Rudolf Steiner developed the principal motif of the sculptural Group in three stages. The first of these was the drawing of the coloured pastel sketch during the Easter period of 1914. It formed the foundation for the implementing of this motif in the eastern part of the small cupola of the first Goetheanum. Because Rudolf Steiner, as already mentioned, was not satisfied with any of his collaborators' attempts at painting, he had to decide to paint this central motif of the entire small cupola himself. The painting work in the building was finally completed after the removal of the scaffolding. At this time Rudolf Steiner was also working on the sculptural Group, where the same motif was to appear in sculptural form. Thus the sculptural Group forms the third stage on the path that has been outlined here.

Behind all three stages, as a theme that weaves through them, stands the battle of Christ with the opposing forces of Lucifer and Ahriman. However, this battle leads not merely to the curbing of their powers but from an esoteric point of view forms the ensuing process of their redemption. Here, too, one can discern certain evolutionary phases leading to this goal. To this end one needs to compare the three works of art that have been mentioned with one another, though in a reverse direction: first the sculptural Group (which remained unfinished), then this same motif in the context of the paintings in the small cupola, and finally the pastel sketch as the seed of the entire development.

In the sculptural Group itself we find barely a trace of a redemption of the adversaries. The appearance of Christ in their midst merely causes them to try to evade this encounter, on the grounds that they are unable to endure His all-permeating power of love. Lucifer hurls himself into the cosmic abyss, breaking his wings, and Ahriman creeps deeply under the surface of the Earth.

In the painting in the small cupola this situation is depicted in a significantly different way. The change mainly concerns the destiny of Lucifer, who is clearly portrayed already in the process of his redemption. No longer does he plunge into the abyss but ascends into the spiritual heights, imitating with his hands the basic gesture of the Representative of Humanity. (With his right hand this is done fairly accurately, whereas it is only partly true of the left.[149]) He seems to be already on his way to become the cosmic pupil of Christ. In this way Lucifer increasingly becomes a being who is entitled to lead man through the cosmic spheres of the spiritual world. He derives the strength that he needs for his transformation from the left, upstretched hand of the Representative of Humanity. One can see above all from the fingers how the rays of light ascend towards Lucifer. This radiating power has its source in the Resurrection of Christ at the Turning Point of Time and is at the same time that of the spiritual Sun, which has been active in the Earth's aura since the Mystery of Golgotha.

However, the fact that Rudolf Steiner continually warns us of the dangers emanating from the luciferic beings leads one to suppose that we are dealing here only with the redemption of a certain portion of luciferic beings, who are gradually becoming the new servants of Christ in the spiritual world.

In contrast, there is no indication of Ahriman's redemption in the painting in the first Goetheanum. As in the sculptural Group, he is in the cupola painting kept imprisoned in the dark (almost black) sphere under the Earth. Nevertheless, one can sense that the spiritual rays of light emanating from the right hand of the Representative of Humanity in Ahriman's direction generate an immense power (see the illustration on p. 112) and, hence, form a kind of precondition for his subsequent redemption.

The whole situation is portrayed completely differently in the pastel sketch. Here the process of Lucifer's redemption (or initially a certain portion of the luciferic spirits) is already complete, as comes to expression above all in that Lucifer is ascending from the heart of Christ into spiritual heights, surrounded by a mighty, fiery red aura in the form of a big cosmic heart. Moreover, his left hand is now open and is pointing upwards, so that he is making the corresponding gesture of the Representative of Humanity his own and is taking it forward.

Lucifer is here depicted as the new Holy Spirit, that is, as a being who henceforth belongs to Christ.[150] 'This Holy Spirit is none other than the resurrected luciferic spirit now risen in a purer, higher glory, the spirit of independent, wisdom-filled knowledge ... The resurrected Lucifer, Lucifer who has now turned to the good, carries the torch aloft before Christ' (GA 107, 22 March 1909). This image of Lucifer who has become the emissary of the Holy Spirit is what is portrayed in the pastel sketch and already indicated in the painting in the small cupola. A process is being enacted here which Rudolf Steiner describes as follows in the same lecture: 'These luciferic beings who have brought man freedom also give him the possibility of now using this freedom in a free way in order to perceive Christ. The luciferic spirits are then purified and cleansed in the fire of Christianity, and the sins that have been inflicted upon the Earth by the luciferic spirits are transformed from a sin into a deed of goodness' (ibid.).

As for Ahriman, one can see from the sketch that he too has begun to follow his redemptive path and is now at its middle stage, comparable with the way that Lucifer is portrayed in the painting in the small cupola. One can recognize that the redemptive process has begun through the fact that Ahriman in the Earth's interior is no longer only surrounded by darkness but is already in the sphere of light that is starting to manifest itself as a kind of extension of the aura of Christ and is filled with the forces of the spiritual Sun, which the Representative of Humanity sends into the depths of the Earth with His right hand. However, the process of redemption is portrayed here only at a very rudimentary stage, more as a delicate hint, which initially probably applies only to a very small portion of ahrimanic beings.[151]

This whole theme can also be understood in an evolutionary time perspective. One thereby acquires a sense of how Rudolf Steiner worked and researched as a spiritual scientist. For spiritual research is carried out through the initiate's immersing himself in the stream of spiritual time, which in the higher worlds flows towards him not out of the past, as does earthly time, but out of the future. Hence in the series of three steps from the pastel sketch to the painting and then to the sculpture, Rudolf Steiner portrayed the sequence of events as it manifests itself to the spirit-researcher directly from the spiritual world. If, however, one would seek to translate what he has thus depicted into earthly time, into an earthly, historical perspective, as it were, one would have to study these three works of art in the opposite sequence, as has been attempted in the present supplement to this book.

Rudolf Steiner. Sketch for the central motif of the small cupola of the first Goetheanum. Pastel on paper, 1914. Compare with the same motif in the painting in the small cupola (p. 6) and in the sculptural Group (frontispiece).

III The Aesthetic Germinal Foundations of the Sculptural Group

If one would seek the aesthetic sources of the sculptural Group in the totality of Rudolf Steiner's work, one has to go right back to the moment when, on 9 November 1888, he unveiled his aesthetic creed in his lecture 'Goethe as the Father of a Science of Aesthetics'.[152]

At the beginning of this lecture Rudolf Steiner emphasizes above all two periods in the history of the West: the golden age of ancient Greece—including the figures of Aristotle and Plato—and medieval Europe.[153] With respect to both epochs he says that aesthetics could not as yet emerge as an independent area of research at the time because the objective preconditions were not in place. These arose only at the end of the eighteenth century, when the first steps towards establishing aesthetics as the science of the beautiful were taken especially in Central Europe by Winckelmann and Lessing. These initial efforts soon found their continuation and culmination in the collaboration between Goethe and Schiller. It was pre-eminently Schiller who, through the example of Goethe, in whom he perceived the archetypal picture of a true artist, was able to establish a complete system of aesthetics in his *Letters concerning Aesthetic Education*. According to Rudolf Steiner 'they are among the most important things to have emerged from the study of aesthetics' (GA 271, 9 November 1888).

Anyone wishing to develop the science of aesthetics further in accordance with the times must—in the opinion of the 27-year-old Rudolf Steiner—form a connection with the achievements of Schiller and Goethe in this regard. In contrast to this were the aesthetic views of, in particular, two great philosophers who dominated and wielded a lasting influence over the intellectual life of Europe in the post-Goethean age. The philosophers he had in mind were Schelling and Hegel, whose views on aesthetics Rudolf Steiner strongly opposed (although he fully recognized their contributions in other areas of philosophy). For a future aesthetics and, hence, also the development of art itself should by no means follow these two philosophers but clearly and unambiguously their predecessors (Schiller and Goethe). And then comes the central message of Rudolf Steiner's lecture, which he formulated out of the polarity of these two trends in aesthetics and by means of which he indicated how art needs to develop if it is to find a source of inspiration through having a new connection with the spiritual world.

Rudolf Steiner describes the two aesthetic standpoints in connection with Goethe's adage 'Consider what thou will'st: still more consider how thou will'st' (*Faust*, Part 2) and comes down firmly on the ground of the second: 'This clearly describes what art is about: not the embodying something of a supersensible nature but the transforming of everyday, sensory life. Something belonging to the real world should not become merely a means of expression; it simply needs to acquire a new form' (ibid.). This is not to say that the physical, material world is drawn down into being a mere garment, in which the idea appears to sensory perception and, hence, becomes merely a symbolic interpretation of the spirit, but that the material is taken hold of and transformed by the artist in such a way that matter itself takes on a spiritual quality.

Later on in his lecture Rudolf Steiner formulates this new orientation of art—deriving from the same polarity—still more precisely: 'This is not the "idea in the form of a sensory manifestation"; rather is it the complete opposite, a "sensory manifestation in the form of the idea". The content of the beautiful, the material substance that underlies it, is, therefore, always a real entity, something that has a direct influence, and the form of its appearance is the ideal ... The beautiful is not the divine in a sense-perceptible aspect; no, it is the sense-perceptible in a divine aspect' (ibid.). And now comes the decisive sentence: 'The artist does not bring the divine to the Earth by letting it flow into the world but by raising the world [down to its material substance] into the sphere of divinity' (ibid.). Only if the artist follows this latter path faithfully and without compromise does he become one who 'furthers the development of the world spirit'. In this way the 'cosmic mission of the artist' is rooted in reality (ibid.).

If one would seek to understand the full consequences of what the young Rudolf Steiner was saying, one must at this point ask two decisive questions. What are the highest and most complete manifestations of the first and of the second of the two aesthetic principles that have been considered here in the history of mankind? What would it signify from the standpoint of world history in the former case if the highest idea or the highest Spirit from the supersensible worlds would unite with a human body? (In the first quotation Rudolf Steiner even uses the words 'an embodying'.) It was precisely this that happened at the Turning Point of Time at the Baptism in the Jordan, when the highest Spirit of the supersensible worlds, the Christ, united with the body of Jesus of Nazareth. Hence one can say that the whole previous evolution of the mysteries of mankind had the task of preparing for this moment, which had been its aim from the outset. This event was indeed the greatest in the whole of human history before the Mystery of Golgotha.

If in the same way one raises the second aesthetic principle, in which Rudolf Steiner recognizes the future of art, to a similar height and then asks where in human history one finds its highest realization, namely a material substance which has been transformed in such a way that it can appear as an idea (thought) or as a pure spirit, one comes to what was achieved by Christ for the entire future of human evolution in the Mystery of Golgotha. This is the Resurrection body, in which earthly matter becomes spirit or a real thought. Hence for Rudolf Steiner the phantom of Christ is 'the real thought' (GA 131, 10 October 1911) and at the same time the perfect 'spirit body', which while continuing to have the qualities of a body (GA 131, 12 October 1911) has nevertheless a spirit being able to pass through physical objects, as is also indicated in the Gospels. (See John 20:19 and 26.)

The esoteric background of the lecture of the young Rudolf Steiner that has been referred to now gradually becomes more understandable. In his dispute with the dominant stream in aesthetics, which even today—in so far as an artist takes the spiritual world into account at all and seeks access to it—continues to be the prevailing one, Rudolf Steiner was quite decisive in not wanting to make a connection with Epiphany as the fulfilment of the whole of pre-Christian evolution but with the Resurrection in the Mystery of Golgotha as the seed for the future of mankind and the Earth. This is the secret and unspoken message that stands esoterically behind the lecture 'Goethe as the Father of a New Science of Aesthetics'.

This is the real reason why in September 1909, after he had laid the foundations of anthroposophy and prepared the book *An Outline of Occult Science* in manuscript form, Rudolf Steiner let this lecture be reprinted without making any changes in its content.[154] In his foreword Rudolf Steiner uses this as an opportunity to emphasize once more that there can be no question of speaking of a break in his inner development, since he would not otherwise have been able to republish this pre-anthroposophical lecture unaltered in his anthroposophical period of creativity. He writes in this regard: 'And if one would seek a dramatic change in my ideas as a result of my spiritual-scientific—anthroposophical—endeavours, it can by way of explanation be said that, on reading through this lecture, I now find that the ideas presented in it would appear to be a sure foundation for anthroposophy. Yes, it even seems to me that an anthroposophical way of conceiving the world is just what is needed for understanding these ideas ... What lay behind my world of ideas 20 years ago has since then been developed by me in all manner of ways; that is the fact of the matter, as distinct from a change in my world conception' (GA 271). That this is indeed the case has been shown in what has already been said. For what underlies this early lecture by Rudolf Steiner can be elucidated if, following his advice, one approaches it with the 'anthroposophical way of conceiving the world' that was developed later and thereby clarifies for oneself by means of this one example the consistency and sense of purpose in Rudolf Steiner's inner development from his youth until the founding of anthroposophy.

Thus Rudolf Steiner basically only needed to follow his aesthetic principle clearly formulated in 1888 consistently and to translate it into artistic forms in order to arrive at what gradually arose during his later activity out of anthroposophy as the new artistic impulse. If one asks oneself which specific artistic forms must arise from a practical application of this aesthetic principle advocated by Rudolf Steiner in his lecture, one can say: If Rudolf Steiner tried to apply this principle whereby the 'sensory manifestation' appears 'in the form of the idea' or of the spirit in specific artistic forms, he would necessarily arrive at precisely what—with respect to his own art—can be called 'spiritual realism'.

Rudolf Steiner made it visually apparent what this actually means in his sculptural Group. For one can see from it how material substance itself has acquired spiritual form in the sense of this aesthetic principle, in that it was indeed possible for the initiate to portray beings of the spiritual world in a manner faithful to the original. And as we have already seen (see chapter 3), both the forms of the Representative of Humanity and also of Lucifer and Ahriman arose on this path as sculptures and paintings.

If one now applies the aforesaid principle to the method of painting employed by Rudolf Steiner above all in the small cupola of the first Goetheanum, we are dealing here not with a symbolic portrayal of spiritual realities in the medium of painting but with the natural birth of spiritual imaginations out of a living tapestry of colours. Thus through this new manner of treatment the colours are spiritualized in such a way that they are enabled to evoke the phenomenological forms of spiritual reality out of themselves. It was in this sense that Rudolf Steiner repainted the southern part of the paintings of the small cupola (including the central motif) with his own hand, because the artists working with him had all carried out their work in too abstract and symbolic a way, in accordance with the artistic principle of Schelling and Hegel.

If, on the basis of photographs that have been preserved, one now compares the painting of the small cupola by Jadwiga and Franciszek Siedlecki, Arild Rosenkrantz and others with what Rudolf Steiner made of it, one gains a very stark sense of the contrast between the two aesthetic principles described above. Or, as one could say more from the perspective of art history: what Rudolf Steiner has painted remains even today, after nigh on a hundred years, timeless and—hence—wholly modern. On the other hand, the efforts of the artists referred to are from a present-day perspective wholly a reflection of their time—whether one classifies them as belonging more to art nouveau, expressionism or symbolism, they simply belong to the artistic trends that generally prevailed at the beginning of the twentieth century.[155]

In connection with the publication of the second edition of the lecture 'Goethe as the Father of a new Science of Aesthetics' in 1909 one needs to bear in mind that in the same year Rudolf Steiner gave the address mentioned earlier for the opening of the branch in Berlin, where he spoke about three pictures which he associated with the same epochs of human evolution to which he had already referred in 1888 (Greece, the Middle Ages and the beginning of the twentieth century). Thus the third of these pictures, which must arise out of the new spiritual inspiration as is manifested in spiritual science, has a direct connection with the content of the lecture of 1888 and also presents the challenge of embodying the aesthetic principle that was formulated there for the first time in actual works of art through the agency of anthroposophy, as Rudolf Steiner was to accomplish in the central motif of the cupola paintings in the first Goetheanum and in the sculptural Group.[156]

If, in conclusion, we return to the highest archetypal pictures of the two fundamental aesthetic principles of the lecture 'Goethe as the Father of a New Science of Aesthetics', that is, on the one hand the Word becoming flesh at the Baptism in the Jordan and, on the other, the flesh becoming Word at the Resurrection of Christ, we find ourselves confronted at the same time by what Rudolf Steiner refers to as the two revelations of Michael to mankind. The first took place shortly after the Turning Point of Time and was recorded by John in the prologue of his Gospel. The other is enacted in our time, when Michael begins his activity as the Time Spirit guiding mankind for the first time since the Mystery of Golgotha.

Rudolf Steiner brings these two revelations together in the following words: 'The Word becoming flesh is the first Michael revelation; the flesh becoming spirit must be the second Michael revelation' (GA 194, 22 November 1919). In this sense the aesthetic principle that Rudolf Steiner established in 1888 brings clear tidings of the second revelation of Michael. And because in our time 'the Michael path ... finds its continuation in the Christ path' (GA 194, 23 November 1919), the direction which the young Rudolf Steiner had prescribed for himself in his lecture also led through all the trials of the turn of the century to his personal experience of Christ,[157] which subsequently found its artistic expression in the sculptural Group and in the corresponding motif of the small cupola.

'If one has a sense of what resides in this figure as the central Being of all earthly evolution, one will be able to discover the Christ.'

Rudolf Steiner[158]

'It was necessary above all else to bring a building into existence which in all its forms is an embodiment of the spiritual being to whom we are devoted.'

Rudolf Steiner[159]

'It is not I, not my own being that makes an impression on the eye through the outer forms [of the building] but the Christ would speak, who seeks an expression, a revelation through a pronouncement of the higher hierarchies. And this building shall be "the mouth"!'

Rudolf Steiner[160]

Rudolf Steiner during his work on the figure of Christ in 1919

Appendix: From the Recollections of Heinz Müller

Heinz Müller (1899–1968), who was one of the original Waldorf teachers, visited Rudolf Steiner in Dornach at the beginning of the 1920s and was in the course of this visit also led before the sculptural Group in the studio, where Rudolf Steiner continued to work on it whenever he had the time available to do so. The explanations that Heinz Müller received there from Rudolf Steiner as they contemplated the Group and its individual forms together are so unusual and unique that they will be reproduced here verbatim.

'In the meantime he had stepped onto a lower platform and was carving the figure of the Representative of Humanity with a broad rounded knife. His right hand was wielding a very large beater with great care; while his left hand was carefully working with the gouge and, as it appeared, with considerable power but also a fair measure of restraint. I now had time to look at a series of sketches for details of the paintings in both cupolas of the Goetheanum. A drawing done using a shading technique of the three Kabieric sacrificial vessels of Samothrace was also there, together with some sketches of both adversaries. After briefly studying the head of Ahriman, the bust of Lucifer and the head of the Representative of Humanity, I proceeded to contemplate the head of Ahriman in greater detail. This rigidly backward inclined, grouchy countenance distorted with mockery and with diagonally slit eyes awoke within me at one and the same time a sense of fear and compassion. Scorn and coldness radiated forth from it, but also—in its whole aspect of negation—the clear will to carry out destructive onslaughts against the world and humanity.

'Rudolf Steiner now put his tool aside and came up to me. First he spoke about the head of Ahriman. If lovelessness, philistinism and pedantry, which have unfortunately become increasingly widespread among many people today, were to achieve a dominant role, all individual characteristics would be lost. Yes, people would become increasingly similar to Ahriman even in the details of their facial features, but also in the configuration of their hands and feet and—ultimately—their entire form. Present-day humanity would need to try to develop clear conceptions of the adversarial forces and in this way wrest their power from them. For this reason he had also endeavoured—so he said—to make his portrayal of them as exact as possible in all its details. In this way he ensured that his figures were as much of a likeness as possible. As his guest was evidently highly surprised at these words, he followed them up with the further startling remark that he had compelled both Ahriman and Lucifer to sit for him as models. With Ahriman he succeeded only after applying a considerable degree of force, whereas Lucifer adapted himself relatively easily to this situation. While these words were being spoken I was filled with marvelling and reverential thoughts about the greatness of the spirit who was able to say such things as though as a matter of course.

'Rudolf Steiner appeared to sense these thoughts immediately, and gave the conversation what was initially a somewhat lighter note by pointing with a smile at an expansive armchair in which such lofty visitors would be obliged to be seated. I had barely taken this in when he continued to say in his original serious tone that he had kept Ahriman confined to this chair until he had finished his study. Then he—Rudolf Steiner—ended the session, but Ahriman sought revenge by destroying the great crimson window on the western façade of the Goetheanum. At that time this window developed a crack from top to bottom.

'Now I came before the figure of Lucifer, which was already wonderfully sculpted in its full dimensions and in mighty surfaces. In addition to the head and chest this portrayed the arms and winglike shape. However, what was most striking for me was the enigmatic way in which Lucifer's larynx was connected on the one hand with his ears and, on the other, with the strong, wavelike wings extending upwards from the breastbone. Rudolf Steiner saw to it that I first put my observations about the sculpture before me in words with the greatest possible exactitude. Then he said something along the following lines: "You see that a great deal of what you have said about Easter purely out of your reflections about the relationships of speech with hearing and breathing is manifested in the bodily form of Lucifer. This should not alarm you, for Lucifer is fully entitled to be involved with everything pertaining to art." There then followed a series of further descriptions about the relationships between speech and breathing, which entered to such an extent into the medical realm that doctors would be better qualified to give a report of them than a teacher.

'There were then further observations about the true likeness of the model of Lucifer. But then Rudolf Steiner saw that his listener was trying to imitate the gestures of Lucifer and Ahriman with his hands and fingers. He offered me help in the following way. He picked up a coffee cup which was standing there, took hold of it very delicately by the handle with his thumb and forefinger, lowered his two middle fingers a little and extended his little finger upward and to the side in an inimitably charming and coquettish way. Then he asked with a merry twinkle in his eyes where and in whom one might often observe this hand gesture. This caused the young *Wandervogel* to make the somewhat impertinent answer that one might well see such a gesture being made by many ladies in the canteen. Rudolf Steiner initially reacted to this observation with evident pleasure but then immediately toned it down and said that he had in mind women getting together and chatting over coffee, with their tendency to demolish all and everything with an overwhelmingly critical sense. Then he added in a kindly way that something of this kind was probably barely to be found in the vicinity of the Goetheanum.

'How completely differently—he pointed out—are the fingers deployed in Ahriman's gout-hardened hands! The thumb and forefinger form as it were an open pair of pincers, while the three other fingers are bent stiffly downwards. A brutal will is expressed in this gesture, explained Rudolf Steiner. In contrast, the hand gesture of the Representative of Humanity is indicative of a harmony between the three soul forces of thinking, feeling and will. In the extension of the forefinger and middle finger vertically upwards, the stretching of the other two fingers forwards below the 90 degree level and the pointing of the thumb in the last of the three dimensions of space, one would have to recognize how in the future the forces of thinking, feeling and will must live independently and yet in mutual harmony.[161] One needs to keep a careful eye on the one-sidedness of gestures and expressions. He also spoke in his observations of legal uses in judgements, that under certain circumstances the downwards pointing thumb could even express the judgement of death. But in the case of the statue of the Representative of Humanity the gestures of the hands and fingers are a manifestation of the streams of love springing from the heart. Thus one should, moreover, by no means suppose that Lucifer's fall is the result of a hostile impulse from Christ; similarly, Ahriman is bound by everything that has been engendered by way of self-destructive power in his highly intelligent but loveless being.

'Then Rudolf Steiner also spoke about the similarity between his study and the countenance of Christ. If one were to encounter Him in the spiritual world, one's first impression would be that His countenance would change to a surprisingly strong degree with every thought, feeling and will impulse. One would then understand that His opponents and enemies had been made aware that a traitor would have to be found in Judas Iscariot whose task would be to dispel the doubt as to who was the right person; for His disciples were interchangeably similar to Him, especially when in their words and deeds they were filled with the inspiration that they derived from His Being.[162] Now that His Being has been living freely in the etheric heights independent of the body of Jesus of Nazareth, this constant changing of His countenance and, indeed, His whole form has further intensified. Nevertheless, Rudolf Steiner assured me, both the sculpture and the coloured portrayals of the Representative of Humanity have been wrought in such a way that one would immediately recognize Him if one were to meet Him. Thus here too one may speak absolutely of a kind of likeness.

'Rudolf Steiner now returned to where he was working, took hold of the broad, flat gouge and the beater and explained what he meant when he spoke of the double curved surface. By means of a mighty thrust with a chisel, he cut a piece of wood from a piece of work which was as yet completely unfinished but was already secured to a large work bench. This yielded some shavings, the result of the hollowing out process of the chisel. He later referred to this way of working with wood somewhat dismissively as "hacking". Immediately adjacent to this he made an incision, and as he did so one could see how he moved the tool in a screwlike fashion, so that over almost the same section of carving he made a turn of approximately 60 degrees in an anticlockwise direction; while with a third cut he guided the chisel in a screwlike way in a clockwise direction. The second and third cuts comprised many small thrusts of the chisel. But both in the piece of work and also among the shavings themselves one could see that no jerky movements had been made as the carving progressed. Whereas the first cut had a barren and deadening effect, the two next ones with their double curved surface immediately evoked a living, imaginative quality. Rudolf Steiner confirmed this observation and said that in any work being executed in wood one should therefore from the outset pay attention to the double curved surface and guard against the deadening "hacking". He now pointed to the figure of the Representative of Humanity, indicating in how lively a way the double curved surfaces reflected the light. Then he went back to carving the knee of the forward moving figure. The very way that the carving was being done on the one hand necessarily indicated the majestic peace of the advancing figure and, on the other, made its forward movement clearly apparent, for it would not be right for the impression to arise that the Christ was standing still here.'[163]

Notes

1. Lecture of 21 October 1917, quoted by A. Fant, A. Klingborg, A.J. Wilkes, *Rudolf Steiner's Sculpture*, English translation, Rudolf Steiner Press, 1975.
2. Lecture of 15 May 1915 (GA 159).
3. Lecture of 28 February 1921, quoted by H. Raske, *Das Farbenwort. Rudolf Steiners Malerei und Fensterkunst im ersten Goetheanum*, Stuttgart 1983. Published in English by Walter Keller Verlag under the title *The Language of Color in the First Goetheanum*, Dornach 1983. This lecture is available in English in Typescript Z 43, 'The Dornach Building', and in the anthology *Architecture*, Rudolf Steiner Press, 2003.
4. GA 233a, 22 April 1924.
5. At the beginning of the year 1924, Rudolf Steiner wrote in section VI of the essay *Das Goetheanum in seinen zehn Jahren* ('The Goetheanum in its Ten Years'), where he was referring to a possible festive opening of the Goetheanum, quite explicitly: 'It did not happen. The Goetheanum had already died into oblivion' (GA 36).
6. In the esoteric lesson of 27 May 1909 in Berlin Rudolf Steiner says in this regard: 'The only true name of Christ is "I am"; anyone who does not know or understand this and calls Him something different does not know anything about Him at all. "I am" is His only name' (GA 266–I).
7. See further about this in S.O. Prokofieff, *May Human Beings Hear It! The Mystery of the Christmas Conference*, ch. 1, 'Rudolf Steiner's Course of Life in the Light of the Christmas Conference', Temple Lodge, 2004.
8. Albert Steffen, *Meetings with Rudolf Steiner*, the chapter entitled 'A Portrait of Rudolf Steiner' (English translation 1961).
9. In the 22nd chapter of his autobiography, *The Course of My Life* (GA 28), Rudolf Steiner describes how this special power became available to him around his 35th year. Around this time 'a first far-reaching change had begun to take place in my mind'. From then on he was increasingly able to unite both worlds on this side of and beyond the threshold. Through his Christ experience around the turn of the century (see ch. 26 of the same book), this spiritual power that he had acquired was so imbued by the Christ impulse that the founding of all the practical anthroposophical initiatives arising out of pure spiritual research subsequently became possible.
10. Albert Steffen, *Meetings with Rudolf Steiner*, the chapter entitled 'The Last Year of Rudolf Steiner's Life'.
11. See H. Raske, *Das Farbenwort. Rudolf Steiners Malerei und Fensterkunst im ersten Goetheanum*, the chapter entitled 'Das Mittelmotiv in der Malerei'. (See note 3.)
12. In this respect it is symptomatic that at the beginning of the same year Rudolf Steiner also spoke for the first time in Berlin about Ahriman in his polarity to Lucifer and of how Ahriman's power could be overcome only through man's connection with Christ.

13. This is the earliest interpretation of the meaning of *The School of Athens* and probably the only one that is consistent with the idea that Rudolf Steiner considered its principal figures to be Plato and Aristotle; whereas in many later observations he ventured the opinion that the figures are Paul and Dionysius the Areopagite. See regarding this problem also S.O. Prokofieff, *Eternal Individuality. A Karmic Biography of Novalis*, ch. 11, 'Novalis as One of the Supersensible Inspirers of the Modern Science of the Spirit', English translation Temple Lodge, 1992 (especially notes 473 and 475).
14. These three epochs of humanity are perhaps best represented by the following three personalities: Aristotle, Thomas Aquinas (both of whom—depending on one's interpretation—can be found in the frescoes referred to) and Rudolf Steiner.
15. Rudolf Steiner speaks in this connection of the possibility that we 'can raise the whole vocation and task of the spiritual-scientific world movement to a higher sphere through the fact that it is the outward manifestation of that inspiration, that power which Christ has called the Spirit' (GA 107, 22 March 1909).
16. In the lecture of 21 November 1919 Rudolf Steiner remarks: 'You must realize that the Christ impulse can be understood only if one sees it as the impulse of balance between the ahrimanic and luciferic principles, if one incorporates it rightly in the Trinity' (GA 194). And then he continues, summarizing in the same lecture the opposing impulses of Lucifer and Ahriman: 'All this is connected with the mission of Michael in relation to those beings of the higher hierarchies with whom he is connected' (ibid.). And in a somewhat earlier lecture he says in this regard: 'Understanding how Christ stands in the middle between Lucifer and Ahriman is one of the main tasks of the immediate future' (GA 165, 9 January 1916). By 'the immediate future' one may best imagine the two and a half centuries that remain of the present Michael epoch.
17. Regarding the present and the two future supersensible revelations of Christ, see S.O. Prokofieff, *The Appearance of Christ in the Etheric. Spiritual-Scientific Aspects of the Second Coming*, ch. 1, 'The Cosmic Dimension of Christ's Second Coming', English translation Temple Lodge, 2012.
18. According to spiritual science an Angel possesses a fully developed Spirit Self, which has a direct relationship to the Holy Spirit.
19. In many places in his lectures Rudolf Steiner speaks of how in modern times an increasing number of people are able to work within their souls on the redemption of Lucifer out of the power of Christ: 'Man will redeem Lucifer if in the corresponding way he takes the power of Christ into his being' (GA 110, 18 April 1909–II). The redemption of Ahriman, on the other hand, is in our time the exclusive preserve of initiates. The concluding words of Benedictus about Ahriman at the end of the fourth Mystery Play testify to this: 'He does not know as yet/that he can be redeemed in future only/ when he can find his being mirrored in/this thinking' (*The Souls' Awakening*, scene XV, GA 14; translation by Adam Bittleston). For other people the first steps towards the redemption of Ahriman are possible only on a path of common (social) spiritual work.
20. GA 143, 8 May 1912. In another lecture Rudolf Steiner says of Christ's brow

that it brings to expression everything 'that one can call wonder at the mysteries of the world' (GA 133, 14 May 1912).

21. F. Rittelmeyer, *Rudolf Steiner Enters My Life*, English translation, Floris Books 1929/1982.
22. See also P. Selg, *Edith Maryon. Rudolf Steiner und die Dornacher Christus-Plastik*, Dornach 2006.
23. What is meant here is the room in the Schreinerei [carpentry workshop] which is immediately adjacent to the high studio. Rudolf Steiner was to spend the last months of his life there on his deathbed.
24. A. Turgeniev, *Reminiscences of Rudolf Steiner and the Work on the First Goetheanum*, the chapter entitled 'The Statue of the "Group"', English translation Temple Lodge, 2003. In her memoirs Assya Turgeniev made the following observations about Edith Maryon's collaboration with the models of the sculptural Group, which consisted above all in the 'preliminary work' referred to: 'In several of her studies one could appreciate the great effort that had been expended by Miss Maryon on the figure of the Representative of Humanity... The strength and ability of Miss Maryon in modelling the various figures was admirable. Only the central figure was not to my liking' (ibid.). For only Rudolf Steiner was able to sculpt this one. Friedrich Rittelmeyer likewise reported in his recollections: 'At that time there was only a bust of Christ in plasticine which Rudolf Steiner had finally modelled himself' (F. Rittelmeyer, *Rudolf Steiner Enters My Life*).
25. This is how it was communicated to the author by Marjorie Spock (1904–2008). She herself heard Rudolf Steiner speaking these words in 1924 as he stood before the sculpture of Christ in his studio. And already in 1922 Rudolf Steiner said to the Czech anthroposophist Julie Klima, as he was likewise standing before the statue of Christ in his studio: 'This is how I see Him, as He has been in our midst.' (Quoted from J. Klima, 'Erinnerungen an Rudolf Steiner', published in the appendix to the book by Ludwig Polzer-Hoditz, *Erinnerungen an Rudolf Steiner*, Dornach 1985.)
26. Rudolf Steiner, *The Architectural Conception of the Goetheanum*, slide lecture in Bern (GA 290).
27. F. Rittelmeyer, *Rudolf Steiner Enters My Life*.
28. In the slide lecture of 3 July 1918 (GA 181) Rudolf Steiner said to his listeners: 'Ahriman's head, as you see it here, is truly spirit, if I may use the paradoxical expression; but you know how a paradox often arises if one characterizes something in a spiritual way. It is indeed spiritually faithful to the model, artistically true to nature. Ahriman had to "sit" in order that this could be brought into being.'
29. H. Müller, *Spuren auf dem Weg. Erinnerungen* ('Footsteps on the Path. Memories'), Stuttgart 1976.
30. See the previous note. Italics by H. Müller.
31. This fashioning of a 'true likeness'—above all of the central figure—in such a way as it appears in the moment in the spiritual world, that is, out of the *eternal present*, does not—in the sense of Rudolf Steiner's elucidations to Heinz Müller—contradict the fact that one is also dealing here with a portrait in the

historical sense. The following words of Rudolf Steiner testify to this: 'This is how the Christ actually lived in the human being Jesus of Nazareth at the beginning of our era in Palestine ... This is what has been attempted: to create a true likeness of Christ' (GA 194, 13 December 1919).

32. Thus Rudolf Steiner once said to Assya Turgeniev: 'I had to soften many aspects of these figures [of the adversaries], otherwise people would not have been able to bear the sight of them' (A. Turgeniev, *Reminiscences of Rudolf Steiner and the Work on the First Goetheanum*, the chapter entitled 'The Statue of "The Group"').

33. Rudolf Steiner likewise said in passing to Friedrich Rittelmeyer that a quite specific difficulty in the sculpting of Christ's countenance lay in having to try to reproduce in the eyes the expression of infinite compassion and ineffable love that radiated from Christ during His life only by means of a notch.

34. See note 29.

35. This has led to Christ often being portrayed in a similar way to God the Father, with the result that the essential difference between these first two Persons of the Trinity has almost completely disappeared. However, this circumstance has an additional, deeper meaning; for after Christianity had been elevated in the fourth century to the official religion of the Roman Empire, the countenance of Christ increasingly acquired the features of the divine Father, on the grounds that people sought in this way to justify above all the claims of the state and subsequently of the Church to authority.

36. Rudolf Steiner, *The Architectural Conception of the Goetheanum*, slide lecture of 29 June 1921 (GA 290).

37. The *left* side of the Group is here described as from the beholder's perspective.

38. Already much earlier than this (in the summer of 1915) Rudolf Steiner said to Friedrich Rittelmeyer: 'I tried to catch Christ's expression at the moment of the temptation' (F. Rittelmeyer, *Rudolf Steiner Enters My Life*).

39. Raphael portrayed this shared childhood experience in many of his pictures, probably from his unconscious memories. See also S.O. Prokofieff, *Eternal Individuality. A Karmic Biography of Novalis*, ch. 4, 'After the Turning Point of Time', English translation Temple Lodge, 1992.

40. See GA 148, 5 October 1913.

41. See further in S.O. Prokofieff, *Eternal Individuality. A Karmic Biography of Novalis*, ch. 2, 'At the Turning Point of Time'.

42. In another lecture where there is no specific reference to the turn of the millennia, this battle is described as follows: 'There will be many, many terrible storms, and to a large extent the significance of these storms is that the luciferic and ahrimanic battle is being waged against the Christ impulse' (GA 165, 9 January 1916).

43. There was already a premonition of this union in the mysteries of late antiquity. Thus the Eleusinian priests knew the secret that in a higher sense the same Being worked through Apollo and Dionysos. Rudolf Steiner says in this regard: 'If one is granted access to Christ, one finds a Being who is Apollo and Dionysos in a *single* essence' (GA 113, 28 August 1909; italics Rudolf Steiner).

44. See GA 124, 19 December 1910.

45. Assya Turgeniev, *Reminiscences of Rudolf Steiner and the Work on the First Goetheanum*, the chapter entitled 'The Statue of the "Group"'.
46. Ibid.
47. See also S.O. Prokofieff, *Rudolf Steiner and the Founding of the New Mysteries*, ch. 4, 'The Earthly and the Supersensible Goetheanum', second English edition Temple Lodge, 1995.
48. In the lecture of 14 October 1917 (GA 177) Rudolf Steiner speaks of the 'fall of Ahriman'.
49. According to spiritual science, such processes as the casting down of the ahrimanic dragon by Michael are very complex and many-sided. Thus the first fall of the dragon from the spiritual world to the human realm took place a long time ago. (See GA 223, 27 September 1923.) However, this dragon was strengthened to a very considerable degree by the subsequent fall of the spirits of darkness in the second half of the nineteenth century (see GA 177, 14 October 1917) and therefore presented a particular danger to the further evolution of mankind.
50. Regarding the connection of the human 'I' with the heart, see GA 129, 26 August 1911.
51. See also GA 93a, 9 October 1905.
52. See GA 13, the chapter entitled 'Present and Future Evolution of the World and of Mankind'.
53. Rudolf Steiner spoke about the connection of the Asuras with the eighth sphere in an esoteric lesson, of which unfortunately only the very brief notes of a listener have been preserved: 'Asuras. These are beings who strive towards the eighth sphere ... The Asuras exert their influence ... upon man, whom they would draw down into the eighth sphere, thus endeavouring to wrench him away from the advancing thrust of evolution and its goal, the Christ' (GA 266–I, 29 January 1907). The way in which Lucifer and Ahriman can, by working together, tear man away from Christian evolution is depicted in the motif on the left side of the Group.
54. In the same lecture Rudolf Steiner describes how the Asuras, once they have thrust their way into the consciousness soul, are gradually able from there to destroy man's ego: 'One piece after another will be drawn forth from the ego,' with the result that the principal goal of humanity on Earth can no longer be reached; for it is associated with the development of the ego.
55. Regarding this spiritual battle for the human heart, see further in S.O. Prokofieff, *The Encounter with Evil and its Overcoming through Spiritual Science*, English translation Temple Lodge, 1999.
56. See GA 159, 18 May 1915. Elsewhere Rudolf Steiner also says that 'through it [gold] he casts himself in bondage' (GA 157, 10 June 1915).
57. This is in accordance with Rudolf Steiner's free translation. The words from the Letter to the Galatians run as follows: 'It is no longer I who lives, but Christ who lives in me' (2:20). Or in Emil Bock's translation: 'Thus it is not I who lives, but Christ lives in me.'
58. 'The Longing of Souls for the Spirit. A Sign of the Time', lecture by Rudolf Steiner in Dornach on 20 September 1914 (available in Typescript EN 43). See

also P. Selg, *Die Gestalt Christi. Rudolf Steiner und die geistige Intention des zentralen Goetheanum-Kunstwerkes*, Arlesheim 2008.

59. Regarding Rudolf Steiner's connection to the copy of Christ's Ego see further in S.O. Prokofieff, *Rudolf Steiner and the Founding of the New Mysteries*, ch. 2, 'The Great Sun Period', second English edition Temple Lodge, 1994, and S.O. Prokofieff, *May Human Beings Hear It! The Mystery of the Christmas Conference*, ch. 1, 'Rudolf Steiner's Course of Life in the Light of the Christmas Conference', Temple Lodge, 2004.

60. See Rudolf Steiner's words on p. 35.

61. Rudolf Steiner says of this cosmic fire and its connection with anthroposophy: 'The anthroposophical fire which can be ignited within us is but an outcome of the universal cosmic fire, which streams spiritually from the beginning to the end' (GA 152, 1 May 1913). That is, it is directly associated with the apocalyptic Christ who appears in the Revelation of St John as 'the alpha and the omega, the beginning and the end' (Rev. 1:8). A comparison of the wooden sculptural Group with the figure of Christ in the fresco of *The Last Judgement* by Michelangelo (GA 161, 3 April 1915, and GA 157, 10 June 1915) also points in the same direction.

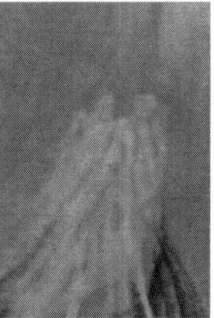

62. The particular gesture of the fingers of the hands of the Representative of Humanity finds its explanation here. It is of such a nature that the cosmic fire of the apocalyptic Christ can stream out of them. It was this 'spiritualized fire' that Paul also saw when he had his Christ experience before Damascus. This can be seen with particular clarity from the pictorial representation of this motif in the eastern part of the small cupola.

63. The letter entitled 'Gnosis and Anthroposophy', January 1925 (GA 26).

64. Or of the young bride with the dead bridegroom in her lap—Sigune with the dead Schionatulander (ibid.).

65. See S.O. Prokofieff, *Rudolf Steiner and the Founding of the New Mysteries*, ch. 7, 'The Michael Epoch and the New Grail Event'.

66. Rudolf Steiner speaks in various places interchangeably about copies of 'Christ's Ego' and 'Christ Jesus's Ego', but sometimes only of the 'ego of Jesus of Nazareth'. The reason for this is that he describes the entire process of the arising of copies of the ego on some occasions from the standpoint of Christ as

an archetype which is its own reflection and, on others, from the standpoint of Jesus, who enables the copy to come about in himself—or from both aspects at the same time, referring as he does so in such a case to Christ Jesus.

67. Here and in what follows the description is from the standpoint of the observer.
68. According to Zeylmans van Emmichoven this line relates to the entelechy of Jesus of Nazareth, which since the Resurrection of Christ has been continuing to work with Him in the spiritual world. See S.O. Prokofieff, 'Die Menschheitsaufgabe der nathanischen Seele', published in the anthology *Gemeinschaftsbildung im Lichte Michaels*, ed. R. Steel, Dornach 2010.
69. The direct connection of the sculptural wooden Group and the painted motif in the small cupola—which was to have been above the place where the Group was to stand in the first Goetheanum—with the fourth part of the Foundation Stone Meditation emerges from the fact that the shepherds, as representatives of the southern mystery stream of the heart, had above all to overcome luciferic forces in themselves on their path to initiation—Gautama Buddha overcoming the demon Mara; and the kings, as the representatives of the northern mystery stream of the head, had above all to battle in their initiation with ahrimanic forces—Zarathustra with Angra Mainyu. Through the radiating power of the 'Sun of Christ' both mystery streams were united on the Earth for the whole future of mankind.
70. Here and for the remainder of this chapter the description is given from the standpoint of the central figure of the sculptural Group.
71. This is apparent from its pronounced asymmetry. Regarding asymmetry as an expression of the etheric, see p. 15.
72. 'Christianity will remain: for whereas in its origins it was a religion, it is greater than all religion! This is Rosicrucian wisdom' (GA 102, 24 March 1908).
73. The extent to which Rudolf Steiner was, in his being and in his initiation, himself existentially connected with these two forces of love and wisdom and embodied and exemplified this 'wisdom warmed through with love' in his life and work is evident from Mario Betti's book *Ein Weg zur Individualität Rudolf Steiners*, Stuttgart 2009.
74. 'The Etherization of the Blood. The Entry of the Etheric Christ into Earthly Evolution' (GA 130, 1 October 1911).
75. Especially in the case of the mighty etheric forms in the heart region of the Representative of Humanity one can gauge how difficult it must have been even for Rudolf Steiner's closest pupils and collaborators rightly to understand what he wanted to express by it on the basis of his spiritual research. Thus there are several studies for the sculptural Group by Edith Maryon where she clothes the figure of Christ in a beautifully folded Roman toga, which possibly Pilate but certainly not Christ might have worn on the Earth. (See the two-metre-high sixth sculptural model for the Group and above all the life-size central figure made of plaster.) Of course, no one but Rudolf Steiner could know that the folds on the chest of the Representative of Humanity had nothing to do with some sort of clothing but, rather, with cosmically human etheric streams. Hence only he had the capacity to fashion not only the countenance but also these etheric forms. For a direct perception of the spiritual world was necessary for this which he alone possessed.

Something similar happened with the painting of the small cupola. The way that the painters conceived of the countenance (and the form) of the Representative of Humanity, and then executed their ideas wholly in the style of the currently fashionable art nouveau, was ultimately so far from Rudolf Steiner's intentions (some sketches and photographs of these original paintings have been preserved) that he removed everything again, took up his brush and had to paint the whole central motif anew with his own hands. Despite the painters' efforts, he was not satisfied with their work. He eventually over-painted all of it, apart from the figure of the Egyptian initiate that Margarita Voloschin had done, which alone harmonized with his intentions.

76. The focus of the two-petalled lotus-flower, which plays a central part in man's initiation and above all in the relationship of his higher ego to the beings of the spiritual world, is at the root of the nose. See Rudolf Steiner, *Knowledge of the Higher Worlds: How is it Achieved?*, the chapter entitled 'Some Effects of Initiation' (GA 10).
77. The three stages of this path from the heart up to the head and then down to the solar plexus at the same time represent the path from the light ether, which streams from the heart through the raised left hand, to the sound ether in the head (and larynx), then to the life ether in the solar plexus and on through the downward stretching right hand. (Regarding the connection between the solar plexus and the life ether, see GA 93a, 26 September 1905.)
78. Regarding the connection of the solar plexus with Old Sun, see GA 99, 2 June 1907.
79. For further insight about the relationship of the heart to the Earth, see GA 243, 13 August 1924.
80. 'While the Earth was Sun, this Spirit [Christ] was the central spirit of the Sun'; and: 'the highest regent, the highest God of the [Old] Sun, the Sun God' was 'Christ' (GA 99, 2 June 1907).
81. Human beings received their etheric bodies on Old Sun.
82. Through the solar plexus Christ was connected on the Earth with Old Sun existence, where He Himself had reached a decisive stage on the path of union with the cosmic Word. (See GA 137, 12 June 1912.)
83. See note 74.
84. GA 13.
85. That is, in the sense of the previous discussion, bringing the battle between the Spirits of Wisdom and the Spirits of Love to a conclusion or victory in one's own heart, in accordance with the example of Christ.
86. 'Left' here is from the observer's standpoint.
87. Regarding the ego-destroying activity of the Asuras, see GA 107, 22 March 1909.
88. Lecture of 29 June 1921 (GA 290).
89. GA 159, 18 May 1915. This theme of a twofold compassion is portrayed on the two side-panels of the northern rose-coloured glass window, where Christ is shown inclining towards Lucifer and Ahriman.
90. The archetypal picture of this influence of Christ is His presence in the Buddhi sphere in the circle of the twelve bodhisattvas. See regarding this also in chapter 14.

91. Maximilian Voloshin wrote these lines on 1 February 1915 in Paris and, hence, nearly half a year before Rudolf Steiner spoke the words quoted above.
92. See further regarding Maximilian Voloshin and his relationship to anthroposophy in S.O. Prokofieff, *Maximilian Woloshin. Mensch, Dichter, Anthroposoph*, Dornach 2007.
93. See GA 120, 19 May 1910.
94. The letter 'Michael's Mission in the Cosmic Age of Human Freedom' (GA 26).
95. Rudolf Steiner says in this regard: 'Naturally, I am not referring to an acute illness, but in our fifth epoch "life" signifies a gradual process of becoming ill' (GA 186, 7 December 1918).
96. See P. Selg, *Krankheit und Christus-Erkenntnis. Anthroposophische Medizin als christliche Heilkunst*, Dornach 2001.
97. In the course of the lecture Rudolf Steiner makes the main directions of this twofold process more concrete. Especially bodily afflictions, which arise through the darkening power of matter, are cured with light-bearing substances from the realm of nature; whereas psychic illnesses are healed more through the soul's capacity for love and sacrifice.
98. Further aspects of this theme can be found in the book by Peter Selg, *Krankheit und Christus-Erkenntnis. Anthroposophische Medizin als christliche Heilkunst*, the chapter entitled 'Vom Leidesfühlen zum Karmawillen', subsection 'Christus, Luzifer und Ahriman—vom Karmawillen', Dornach 2001.
99. Rudolf Steiner associates Parzival's initiation with modern initiation in the fifth post-Atlantean cultural epoch in that he says of it that 'everything that comes to expression in the figure of Parzival, this ideal of modern initiation ... is dependent on the consciousness soul' (GA 144, 7 February 1913).
100. See GA 264.
101. See also S.O. Prokofieff, *The Occult Significance of Forgiveness*, ch. VII, 'The Nature of Forgiveness and the Sevenfold Manichaean Initiation', third English edition Temple Lodge, 1995/2004.
102. See S.O. Prokofieff, *The Encounter with Evil and its Overcoming through Spiritual Science*, part I, English edition Temple Lodge 1999.
103. See also S.O. Prokofieff, *Und die Erde wird zur Sonne. Einige Zusammenhänge des Golgotha-Geschehens aus anthroposophischer Sicht*, ch. 6, 'Vom Weltenschicksal des Bösen', Verlag des Ita Wegman Instituts, 2012.
104. See S.O. Prokofieff, *The Mystery of the Resurrection in the Light of Anthroposophy*, ch. 1, 'The Mystery of Golgotha and Spiritual Communion', English translation Temple Lodge, 2010.
105. In the lecture itself Rudolf Steiner also uses the words 'spiritual communion', which is wholly justified in that cosmic communion by its very nature happens in a purely spiritual way.
106. See note 104.
107. For in order to investigate these cosmic mysteries in the manner described as they are portrayed in the principal figure of the sculptural Group, an initiate—thus Rudolf Steiner—had to free his head from Lucifer and his metabolism from Ahriman by receiving the Christ impulse into his own heart.

108. Rudolf Steiner speaks of how eternity consists of two parts, unborn-ness and immortality, in the lecture of 18 May 1924 (GA 236).
109. This is once again an indirect reference to the activity of the Asuras, who lie behind the *united* efforts of Lucifer and Ahriman. For the activity of the Asuras is directed against man's relationship to the sphere of eternity; and this relationship can only be disturbed if the Asuras manage directly to harm the human ego. (Rudolf Steiner speaks of how this happens in GA 107, 22 March 1909.)
110. See Hilde Raske, *Das Farbenwort. Rudolf Steiners Malerei und Fensterkunst im ersten Goetheanum*, the chapter entitled 'Beziehungen der Fenster zu den malerischen Motiven der kleinen Kuppel'.
111. The letter entitled 'The Michael-Christ Experience of Man' (GA 26, italics Rudolf Steiner).
112. The experience of Christ at the stage of Intuition, as described in the book *Occult Science* (GA 13), also has a connection with the imagery of this window. See further regarding this in S.O. Prokofieff, *The Appearance of Christ in the Etheric*, English edition Temple Lodge, 2012.
113. It must also be supposed that, by the time of the consecration or esoteric opening of the building (which at the time of the fire had not yet taken place), Rudolf Steiner would already have been able to begin his great investigations of karma; for such research would have been fully in harmony with the capacity of the forms of the first Goetheanum to awaken karmic vision.
114. Regarding this pedagogical law see GA 317, 26 June 1924. The relevant words there are: '... and an ego can be influenced only by what is living in a Spirit Self'.
115. In the description of cosmic communion in the lecture of 31 December 1922 the name of Christ is not mentioned. At this time the carving of the sculptural Group was not complete and therefore it had not been placed in the Goetheanum.
116. The other six were as regards their main features already generally familiar from the occult literature of earlier times. (See GA 284.)
117. See Rudolf Steiner, *Die Goetheanum-Fenster. Sprache des Lichtes*, text volume, Assya Turgeniev's introduction to the first edition of 1961.
118. See ibid., Assya Turgeniev's essay on 'Die Goetheanum-Fenstermotive'.
119. The spirals are fiery, formed of the cosmic fire in which Christ is working today. (See p. 32.)
120. See GA 97, 29 April 1906.
121. In the apocalyptic seals the image of the rainbow appears three times. Firstly in the sign of the Father (second seal) still in the form of a circle; then in the sign of the Son as a revelation of the Sun Spirit (fourth seal); while on the seventh seal it stands for the bond with the Spirit.
122. 'World of space', 'rhythms of time', 'grounds of eternity' (GA 260, 25 December 1923).
123. According to Rudolf Steiner, through the Mystery of Golgotha Christ also brought the essential nature of spiritual time to the Earth and revealed this mystery to the disciples after His Resurrection during the 40 days of His conversations with them (Acts 1:3). (See GA 236, 4 June 1924.)

124. The main motifs of the windows in the first Goetheanum were arranged in such a way (and this is also the case in the second Goetheanum) that in order to understand them properly one had to go from one to the other and thereby follow a Caduceus form. See S.O. Prokofieff, *The Twelve Holy Nights and the Spiritual Hierarchies*, ch. 3, 'The Starry Script and the Architectural Conception of the First Goetheanum', second English edition Temple Lodge, 1993/2004, and also S.O. Prokofieff/P. Selg, *Das erste Goetheanum und seine christologischen Grundlagen*, 'Das Wesen des ersten Goetheanum und das Mysterium von Golgatha', Arlesheim 2009; published in English by SteinerBooks 2012 under the title *The Creative Power of Anthroposophical Christology*.
125. The illustration of the seventh apocalyptic seal on p. 72 was painted for the Munich Congress in 1907 by Klara Rettich. The original seals of the Congress have not been preserved. In 1911 she painted all seven seals again at the instigation of Rudolf Steiner, this time for the decoration of the room of the Stuttgart branch of the Society. The stars on the seventh seal can be clearly discerned in this second rendering. (See the reproduction in GA 284/285.)
126. See the illustration on p. 70. The pentagon refers in this sense to the fifth principle of man's being—the Spirit Self (after the physical body, etheric body, astral body and ego)—of which Rudolf Steiner says in his book *Theosophy*: 'The spirit streams into the ego and lives in it as in a "sheath" ... The spirit forming an "ego" and living as the "I" will be called "Spirit Self", because it manifests itself as the "ego" or "self" of man' (GA 9).
127. See the illustration of the seventh seal on p. 72.
128. These words of the new Isis correspond to those which were inscribed above the mysterious secret image of Isis at Sais in the Egyptian epoch: 'I am the all, I am the past, the present and the future; no mortal has yet lifted my veil' (ibid.).
129. The letter entitled 'The Activity of Michael and the Future of Mankind' (GA 26).
130. It is related that during a eurythmy rehearsal in the first Goetheanum a eurythmist had put a small object (a wristwatch or a handbag) on one of the thrones. Rudolf Steiner, who was in the room, noticed this, immediately interrupted the rehearsal and asked for the object to be removed. Afterwards he said with great seriousness that this should never happen again. (This story was recounted to the author by Maria Schuster-Jenny, who had heard it from the mouth of an older eurythmist who had herself been present.)
131. Rudolf Steiner describes in the lecture of 31 August 1909 (GA 113) the high lodge of the twelve bodhisattvas in the Buddhi sphere of the spiritual world (above higher Devachan), where they—as representatives of the entire wisdom of our cosmos—are immersed in a contemplation of the cosmic Christ as the spiritual Sun and the source of the life of the whole world. The way that the small cupola space of the first Goetheanum was formed was intended to manifest (among much else) an earthly reflection of this cosmic imagination. As the forms of the thrones mirrored one another, that is, the six left ones had the same form as the six right ones, they were at a still higher stage expressive of the six Sun Elohim, who together form the essential nature of the Sun Logos. (See GA 103, 20 May 1908.) At the beginning of earthly evolution Christ descended

to the Sun and into their circle from still higher spiritual worlds. ('The Christ descended to the Sun from even more distant heights', GA 211, 24 April 1922.)

132. Thus Rudolf Steiner affirmed to Heinz Müller that 'both the sculpture and the coloured portrayals of the Representative of Humanity were fashioned in such a way that one would immediately recognize Him if one were to meet Him' (Heinz Müller, *Spuren auf dem Weg. Erinnerungen*, Stuttgart 1976).

133. GA 231, 18 November 1923, printed in the notes to the 1982 German edition.

134. Lecture of 29 June 1921 in Rudolf Steiner, *The Architectural Conception of the Goetheanum* (GA 290).

135. Lecture of 3 February 1913 (English translation in Typescript S 11; also included in *Isis Mary Sophia, Her Mission and Ours*, SteinerBooks 2003).

136. Rudolf Steiner also spoke in this respect about a future Michael culture. (See further below.)

137. Lecture of 12 June 1920 in Stuttgart. Quoted from Hilde Raske, op. cit.

138. One can even say that the whole Christmas Conference, where Rudolf Steiner spoke of how every anthroposophist must enliven his heart with the being Anthroposophia (see GA 260, 25 December 1923), stood under the sign of self-knowledge. (See ibid.)

139. See S.O. Prokofieff/P. Selg, *Das erste Goetheanum und seine christologischen Grundlagen*, Arlesheim 2009.

140. That Rudolf Steiner speaks here of a 'picture', of 'depicting' and 'painting' acquires further significance if one thinks of the paintings in the first Goetheanum with the motif of the Representative of Humanity in their midst.

141. GA 112, 30 June 1909.

142. The seven stages of this evolution from Saturn to the future Venus were portrayed in the capitals of the Great Hall, with two capitals—that of Mars and that of Mercury—representing the Earth. The following words of Rudolf Steiner make it clear that this evolutionary sequence is associated with the new revelation of Isis-Sophia in anthroposophy: 'We must have a living picture in our minds of all that we have acquired through the newly found Isis [in the same lecture he also calls her Sophia], so that the whole heavenly world becomes for us imbued with spirit. We must gain an inner understanding of Saturn, Sun, Moon, Earth, Jupiter, Venus and Vulcan' (GA 202, 24 December 1920).

143. See further regarding the question of the three egos of man in S.O. Prokofieff, *Das Rätsel des menschlichen Ich*, Dornach 2010.

144. The lecture was given in Bologna on 8 April 1911 under the title 'The Psychological Foundations of Anthroposophy and its Standpoint in Relation to the Theory of Knowledge', published in GA 35, and also—together with two summaries of essential points from the lecture and other reports—in *Das gespiegelte Ich. Der Bologna Vortrag—die philosophischen Grundlagen der Anthroposophie*, Dornach 2007.

145. See note 143.

146. See GA 165, 19 December 1915.

147. See further in GA 114, 18 and 19 September 1909.

148. For further thoughts regarding these problems see also S.O. Prokofieff, *What is Anthroposophy?*, English edition Temple Lodge, 2006.

149. In contrast to the Representative of Humanity the left hand of Lucifer is not fully extended, his fingers are not completely opened out to what is above and, hence, are not fully permeable by the power of Christ.
150. Both here and in the quotation cited below the Holy Spirit is referred to not as the third aspect of the Trinity but as it manifests itself in the realm of the Angels, who represent the principle of the Holy Spirit within the Third Hierarchy. For the luciferic spirits are Angels who remained behind on Old Moon and who have thereby lost the possibility of being messengers of the Holy Spirit for people on Earth.
151. Rudolf Steiner depicted the inner process of the redemption of Lucifer and Ahriman through Christ's influence in the Earth's aura after the Resurrection on both side panels of the northern rose-coloured window. (In the second Goetheanum this motif was executed by Assya Turgeniev in a manner faithful to Rudolf Steiner's indications.)
152. The lecture was given to the Goethe Society in Vienna and published shortly afterwards.
153. Rudolf Steiner does not mention any particular names in connection with the Middle Ages. However, he reported subsequently that the Catholic Father Wilhelm Neumann (1837–1919) spoke to him after the lecture and said: 'The seeds for this lecture that you gave us today are to be found in Thomas Aquinas!' (GA 74, 24 May 1920).
154. Rudolf Steiner provided this second edition of the lecture with some notes, in the last of which he formulates in somewhat different words the task of every true artist whom is called to create something new in the world: 'The sensory reality will be transfigured in art through being manifested as spirit. In this respect artistic creation is not an imitation of something already in existence but a means of taking the world process forward arising from the human soul. The mere imitation of the natural world is just as little the creation of something new as is the forming of an image of an already existing spirit' (GA 271).
155. In the exhibition 'Im Schwingungszustand des Lebens. Der Mensch zwischen Luzifer und Ahriman' (In the Oscillatory Turbulence of Life. Man between Lucifer and Ahriman), which could be seen at the Goetheanum between 27 February and 17 April 2011 in commemoration of the 150th anniversary of Rudolf Steiner's birth, one could clearly find confirmation of this for oneself.
156. It is striking to discover that already in the lecture of 1888, thus at the very beginning of his lecturing activity, Rudolf Steiner mentions Aristotle (albeit in a critical sense) and then, after he had finished his lecture, referred to Thomas Aquinas. (See note 153.) Thus at a very early stage the path was indicated that leads from Aristotle to Thomas Aquinas and then to Rudolf Steiner himself. (See also Thomas Meyer, *Rudolf Steiner's Core Mission. The Birth and Development of Spiritual-Scientific Karma Research*, English translation Temple Lodge, 2010.) Then the same threefold succession appears again in 1909 at the opening of the branch in Berlin, where in connection with Raphael's 'Stanzas' a link was made with Aristotle and Plato in the *School of Athens* and with the Middle Ages through the *Disputa*, where Thomas Aquinas and Dante are portrayed (although he does not mention them by name). And then, as a third step, there

is a reference to the picture to be created in the future, which must arise out of the spirit of anthroposophy. This series of three stages appears on a further occasion in the lecture of 3 February 1913, likewise in Berlin, in the course of the description of the passage of the supersensible being Anthroposophia through the cultural history of the West. Here too there was a brief description of the flowering of Greek culture and then of the Middle Ages, with Dante cited as its chief protagonist (he was influenced especially by the teachings of Thomas Aquinas when he was writing his *Divine Comedy*). After this there is a description of how at the third stage this supersensible being herself appears in anthroposophy through the mediation and creative power of Rudolf Steiner. It follows from these connections that we may see a direct inspiration of the being Anthroposophia both in the lecture of 1888 and also in that of 1909: the first lecture still from the realm of the consciousness soul and the second—associated as it was with the task of creating the third picture—already from the realm of the Spirit Self, as Rudolf Steiner describes it in the lecture of 3 February 1913. (This lecture was published for the first time by Marie Steiner in the anthology *Schicksalszeichen auf dem Entwicklungswege der Anthroposophischen Gesellschaft* (Signs of Destiny on the Developmental Path of the Anthroposophical Society), Dornach 1943.) Regarding the connection both of the sculptural Group and also of the corresponding motif in the paintings of the small cupola with the being Anthroposophia, see chapter 15 of this book.

157. See chapter XXVI of his autobiography, *The Course of My Life* (GA 28).
158. See note 3, lecture of 25 January 1920.
159. 'Regarding the Johannesbau [St John's Building] in Dornach', address in Vienna before the lecture on 14 April 1914 (GA 153).
160. 'The Longing of Souls for the Spirit. A Sign of the Time', lecture by Rudolf Steiner in Dornach on 20 September 1914.
161. It is striking that the description of the finger positions of the hand of the Representative of Humanity that Rudolf Steiner gave to Heinz Müller by way of an explanation differs from how he eventually executed them in the sculptural Group. The difference consists in the positions of the forefinger and middle finger, which do not point vertically upwards but are bent forward at a 90 degree angle, as are the two other ones. Rudolf Steiner explained this unusual position of the fingers somewhat differently in conversation with the Czech anthroposophist Julie Klima: ' I asked the master why the fingers of the Christ's hands are divided in so distinctive a way. He answered with a visible joy, while raising both hands in this way: "This is how Jewish initiates gave their blessings." ' (Quoted from J. Klima, 'Erinnerungen an Rudolf Steiner', published in the appendix to the book by Ludwig Polzer-Hoditz, *Erinnerungen an Rudolf Steiner*, Dornach 1985.) This gesture of blessing of the Jewish initiates goes back to Melchizedek, who blessed Abraham in this way in the name of the Most High God (Genesis 14:19). In the case of this gesture all five fingers form a kind of protective and orientating environment for the source of the light and power radiating from the middle of the palm of the hand. One can also experience this radiating power in the gestures of the hands of the Representative of Humanity. This

can be clearly discerned in the painted version of this motif in the small cupola of the first Goetheanum.
162. Rudolf Steiner speaks in a lecture from the Fifth Gospel about this unique presence of Christ in His disciples, which had the effect that no one else was able to know exactly where Christ Jesus Himself actually was. (See GA 148, 6 October 1913.)
163. From Heinz Müller, *Spuren auf dem Weg. Erinnerungen* ('Footsteps on the Path. Memories'), Stuttgart 1976, pp. 38–41. Italics by Heinz Müller.

Bibliography

Quotations from the Bible are taken from the Revised Standard Version.

Words or phrases in italics are—except where indicated otherwise—emphases by the author.

The following list of Rudolf Steiner's works comprises the writings and lectures cited in the present book and is arranged in accordance with the volumes of the Collected Works (Gesamtausgabe or GA). Where a German title is given, this means that the volume concerned has not been translated or that the lectures are included in more than one published book. Where this is the case, indications are given as to where individual lectures quoted or referred to in this book that have been translated may be found. Translations from Rudolf Steiner's books and lectures in the present volume have, with a few exceptions, been made or edited by the translator.

GA 9	*Theosophy*
GA 10	*Knowledge of the Higher Worlds/How to Know Higher Worlds*
GA 13	*Occult Science/An Outline of Esoteric Science*
GA 14	*Four Mystery Plays*
GA 15	*The Spiritual Guidance of Man and Humanity*
GA 17	*The Threshold of the Spiritual World*
GA 21	*The Riddles of the Soul*
GA 26	*Anthroposophical Leading Thoughts*
GA 28	*The Story of My Life/The Course of My Life/Autobiography*
GA 30	*Methodische Grundlagen der Anthroposophie* The lecture of 9 November 1888 is included in *Art*.
GA 35	*Philosophie und Anthroposophie* The lecture of 8 April 1911 is included in *Esoteric Development* and *Seeing with the Soul*.
GA 36	*Der Goetheanumgedanke inmitten der Kulturkrisis der Gegenwart*
GA 74	*Die Philosophie des Thomas von Aquino* The lecture of 24 May 1920 is included in *The Philosophy of Thomas Aquinas/The Redemption of Thinking*.
GA 84	*Was wollte das Goetheanum und was soll die Anthroposophie?* The lecture of 9 April 1923 is available in Typescript S 34, 'What was the Purpose of the Goetheanum?'
GA 93a	*Foundations of Esotericism*
GA 96	*Ursprungsimpulse der Geisteswissenschaft* The lecture of 1 April 1907 is available in *Original Impulses for the Science of the Spirit*
GA 97	*The Christian Mystery*
GA 99	*Theosophy of the Rosicrucian* or *Rosicrucian Wisdom*
GA 102	*The Influence of Spiritual Beings on Man*

GA 103	*The Gospel of St John*
GA 104	*The Apocalypse of St John*
GA 107	*Geisteswissenschaftliche Menschenkunde*
	The lecture of 22 March 1909 is included in *The Deed of Christ and the Opposing Spiritual Powers*
GA 109	*The Principle of Spiritual Economy* or *Rosicrucian Esotericism*
GA 110	*The Spiritual Hierarchies and their Reflection in the Physical World*
GA 112	*The Gospel of St John in its Relation to the Other Gospels*
GA 113	*The East in the Light of the West*
GA 114	*The Gospel of St Luke*
GA 120	*The Manifestations of Karma*
GA 129	*Wonders of the World, Ordeals of the Soul, Revelations of the Spirit*
GA 130	*Esoteric Christianity*
GA 131	*From Jesus to Christ*
GA 132	*Inner Realities of Evolution*
GA 133	*Earthly and Cosmic Man*
GA 137	*Man in the Light of Occultism, Theosophy and Philosophy*
GA 143	*Erfahrungen des Übersinnlichen. Die drei Wege der Seele zu Christus*
	The lecture of 8 May 1912 is included in *The Artistic Representation of Christ*.
GA 144	*The Mysteries of the East and of Christianity*
GA 147	*Secrets of the Threshold*
GA 148	*The Fifth Gospel*
GA 149	*Christ and the Spiritual World and the Search for the Holy Grail*
GA 152	*Approaching the Mystery of Golgotha*
GA 153	*The Inner Nature of Man and the Life between Death and a New Birth*
GA 157	*Destinies of Individuals and of Nations*
GA 159	*Das Geheimnis des Todes*
	The lecture of 18 May 1915 is published under the title *Christ in Relation to Lucifer and Ahriman*. (That of 15 May 1915 is not translated.)
GA 161	*Wege der geistigen Erkenntnis und der Erneuerung künstlerischer Weltanschauung*
	The lecture of 3 April 1915 is included in *Festivals of the Seasons*.
GA 165	*Die geistige Vereinigung der Menschheit durch den Christus-Impuls*
	The lecture of 19 December 1915 is included in *Festivals of the Seasons* and published under the title *The Christmas Thought and the Mystery of the Ego*.
	The lecture of 9 January 1916 appeared in the *Anthroposophical Quarterly* no. 15:4 under the title 'The Spiritual Unity of Mankind' and is also published separately as *The Universal Human*.
GA 177	*The Fall of the Spirits of Darkness*
GA 180	*Mysterienwahrheiten und Weihnachtsimpulse. Alte Mythen und ihre Bedeutung.*
	The lecture of 6 January 1918 is included in *Ancient Myths—Their Meaning and Connection with Evolution*.
GA 181	*Erdensterben und Weltenleben. Anthroposophische Lebensgaben. Bewusst-*

Bibliography

	seins-Notwendigkeiten für Gegenwart und Zukunft
	The lecture of 3 July 1918 can be found in Typescript C 50, 'A Sound Outlook for Today'.
GA 184	*Die Polarität von Dauer und Entwickelung im Menschenleben*
	The lecture of 21 September 1918 is included in Typescript Z 362, 'The Cosmic Prehistoric Ages of Mankind'.
GA 186	*The Challenge of the Times*
GA 191	*Soziales Verständnis aus geisteswissenschaftlicher Erkenntnis*
	The lecture of 4 November 1919 is included in *Influences of Lucifer and Ahriman*.
GA 194	*The Mission of the Archangel Michael*
GA 202	*Die Brücke zwischen der Weltgeistigkeit und dem Physischen des Menschen*
	The lectures of 23 and 24 December 1920 can be found in *The Search for the New Isis*.
GA 204	*Materialism and the Task of Anthroposophy*
GA 211	*The Sun Mystery*
GA 219	*Man and the World of Stars*
GA 223	The lecture of 27 September 1923 forms part of the lecture cycle entitled *Michaelmas and the Soul Forces of Man*.
GA 229	*The Four Seasons and the Archangels*
GA 231	*Supersensible Man*
GA 233	*World History in the Light of Anthroposophy*
GA 233a	The lecture of 22 April 1924 is included in *The Easter Festival in relation to the Mysteries*.
GA 236	*Karmic Relationships vol. II*. The lecture of 4 June 1924 is, however, included in *The Festivals and their Meaning*.
GA 240	*Karmic Relationships vols VI and VIII*. The lecture of 21 August 1924 is in volume VIII.
GA 243	*True and False Paths in Spiritual Investigation*
GA 254	*The Occult Movement in the Nineteenth Century*
GA 260	*The Christmas Conference*
GA 261	*Unsere Toten*. The memorial address on 3 May 1924 can be found in Typescript S 33, 'Addresses at the memorials of Mme. Ferrari and Edith Maryon'.
GA 264	*From the History and Contents of the First Section of the Esoteric School, 1904–1914*
GA 266–I–III	*Esoteric Lessons, 1904–1914*
GA 271	*Kunst und Kunsterkenntnis*
	The lecture of 9 November 1888 (see GA 30) is also included in this volume.
GA 284	*Rosicrucianism Renewed*
GA 286	*Architecture as a Synthesis of the Arts*
GA 290	The lecture of 29 June 1921 is available under the title *The Architectural Conception of the Goetheanum*.
GA 307	*A Modern Art of Education*
GA 317	*Education for Special Needs*

Further Literature on the Theme of the Book

Åke Fant, A. Klingborg, A.J. Wilkes, *Rudolf Steiner's Sculpture in Dornach*, English edition Rudolf Steiner Press, 1975

Hilde Raske, *The Language of Color in the First Goetheanum*, English edition Walter Keller Verlag, Dornach 1983

Hagen Biesantz, Arne Klingborg, *The Goetheanum. Rudolf Steiner's Architectural Impulse*, English edition Rudolf Steiner Press, 1979

Rex Raab, *Edith Maryon. Bildhauerin und Mitarbeiterin Rudolf Steiners*, Dornach 1993

Peter Selg, *Die Gestalt Christi. Rudolf Steiner und die geistige Intention des zentralen Goetheanum-Kunstwerkes*, Arlesheim 2008

Peter Selg, *Edith Maryon, Rudolf Steiner und die Dornacher Christus-Plastik*, Dornach 2006

Credits and copyright details for illustrations

© Michael Schnur	ii
© Verlag am Goetheanum, Dornach/Schweiz	vi
© Verlag am Goetheanum, Dornach/Schweiz	6
© Rudolf Steiner Nachlassverwaltung, Dornach/Schweiz	9
Picture 1 © Verlag am Goetheanum, Dornach/Schweiz, Picture 2 und 4 © Rudolf Steiner Nachlassverwaltung, Dornach/Schweiz, Picture 3 © Archiv am Goetheanum, Dornach/Schweiz	13
© Verlag am Goetheanum, Dornach/Schweiz	14
© Archiv am Goetheanum, Dornach/Schweiz	40
© Verlag am Goetheanum, Dornach/Schweiz	41
© Verlag am Goetheanum, Dornach/Schweiz	44
Drawing by Sergej O. Prokofieff ©	45
Drawing by Sergej O. Prokofieff ©	70
© Rudolf Steiner Nachlassverwaltung, Dornach/Schweiz	72
© Verlag am Goetheanum, Dornach/Schweiz	74
© Kunstsammlung Goetheanum	94
© Archiv am Goetheanum, Dornach/Schweiz	101
© Verlag am Goetheanum, Dornach/Schweiz	112

By the same author:

Anthroposophy and The Philosophy of Freedom
The Appearance of Christ in the Etheric
The Creative Power of Anthroposophical Christology (with Peter Selg)
Crisis in the Anthroposophical Society and Pathways to the Future (with Peter Selg)
The Cycle of the Seasons and the Seven Liberal Arts
The Cycle of the Year as a Path of Initiation
The East in the Light of the West, Parts One to Three
The Encounter with Evil and its Overcoming through Spiritual Science
The Esoteric Significance of Spiritual Work in Anthroposophical Groups
Eternal Individuality, Towards a Karmic Biography of Novalis
The Foundation Stone Meditation
The Guardian of the Threshold and The Philosophy of Freedom
The Heavenly Sophia and the Living Being Anthroposophia
May Human Beings Hear it!
The Mystery of John the Baptist and John the Evangelist
The Mystery of the Resurrection in the Light of Anthroposophy
The Occult Significance of Forgiveness
Prophecy of the Russian Epic
Relating to Rudolf Steiner
Rudolf Steiner and the Founding of the New Mysteries
Rudolf Steiner's Research into Karma and the Mission of the Anthroposophical Society
The Spiritual Origins of Eastern Europe and the Future Mysteries of the Holy Grail
The Twelve Holy Nights and the Spiritual Hierarchies
What is Anthroposophy?
Why Become a Member of the Anthroposophical Society?
Why Become a Member of the School of Spiritual Science?
The Whitsun Impulse

The Case of Valentin Tomberg
Valentin Tomberg, Rudolf Steiner and Anthroposophy